MACDONALD LEISURE SERIES

Art in London

A Guide to some of the World's finest Paintings

Brian Dobbs

Foreword by Sir John Rothenstein

MACDONALD AND JANE'S · LONDON

Acknowledgments

We would like to thank the following for their permission to reproduce the paintings that appear in this book: The Courtauld Institute Galleries (*Bar at the Folies-Bergère* by Manet); The Greater London Council as Trustees of The Iveagh Bequest, Kenwood (*Portrait of the Painter in Old Age* by Rembrandt); the National Gallery, London (*The Supper at Emmaus* by Caravaggio, *The Baptism of Christ* by Piero della Francesca and *The Arnolfini Marriage* by Jan Van Eyck); The Tate Gallery, London (*Newton* by Blake, *The Roast Beef of Old England ('Calais Gate')* by Hogarth and *Whaam*! by Roy Lichtenstein); The Victoria and Albert Museum (*The Miraculous Draught of Fishes* by Raphael); The Trustees of the Wallace Collection (*The Swing* by Fragonard).

First published 1975 by Macdonald and Jane's,
Macdonald & Co. (Publishers) Ltd.,
Paulton House,
8 Shepherdess Walk,
London N1 7LB.

cased edition ISBN 0 356 08195 8
paperback edition ISBN 0 356 08194 x

printed in Great Britain by
Tinling (1973) Ltd., Prescot, Merseyside
(a member of the Oxley Printing Group Ltd.)

Contents

Foreword

Introduction

1 TRAFALGAR SQUARE AND WHITEHALL
The National Gallery 1
The National Portrait Gallery 17
Institute of Contemporary Arts 22
The Banqueting House, Whitehall 22

2 MILLBANK
The Tate Gallery 29

3 GOING WEST FROM PICCADILLY
The Royal Academy 41
The Museum of Mankind 41
Apsley House – The Wellington Museum 42
The Queen's Gallery 46
The London Museum – a special note 47
Leighton House 48

4 SOUTH KENSINGTON
The Victoria and Albert Museum 53

5 WEST CENTRAL
The British Museum 63
The Thomas Coram Foundation and Foundling Hospital 68
Sir John Soane's Museum 69
The Courtauld Galleries 73
The Wallace Collection 77

6 FURTHER AFIELD
The Imperial War Museum 87
The Hayward Gallery 89

A Trip to Hampstead
(i) *Fenton House* 89
(ii) *Kenwood* 91
The Dulwich College Picture Gallery 93
A Trip to Chiswick 96
(i) *Hogarth House* 97
(ii) *St Nicolas' Parish Church* 97
(iii) *Chiswick House* 98
William Morris Gallery and Brangwyn Gift 99
A Trip to Greenwich 101
(i) *The Royal Naval College Painted Hall and Chapel* 101
(ii) *The National Maritime Museum* 103
Syon House 104
Ham House 106
Osterley Park House 110
The Royal Holloway College 113
Hampton Court Palace 115
Windsor Castle 119

7 BOND ST AND ST JAMES'S
The Commercial Art Galleries 125

Appendix One: SOME ART BOOKSHOPS 135

Appendix Two: AN INDEX OF ARTISTS REPRESENTED IN LONDON COLLECTIONS 136

INDEX TO MUSEUMS AND GALLERIES 153

Foreword

London possesses some of the finest collections of paintings and drawings anywhere. Rome, for obvious reasons, offers unrivalled examples, besides much else, of the giants of the Italian renaissance. And New York, during the past century, thanks to the perceptiveness and wealth as well as the public spirit of a large number of patrons, has assembled collections of outstanding splendour; while Paris of course, has long enjoyed a foremost place for its collections. But no city surpasses London for the splendour and range of its collections; with the National and Tate Galleries, the British Museum, the Victoria and Albert Museum, the Wallace Collection, the more recently established Courtauld Gallery and a number of other institutions. These, however, through booklets, catalogues, advertisements and occasionally films, provide information about their possessions and activities.

In this highly informative volume these world-famous collections are far from neglected, but there are two respects in which it is of particular value. It draws attention to the considerable number of institutions which possess works of the highest quality, yet are often overlooked – owing in some cases to their location, to absence of promotion or to some other cause. Who, for instance, apart from scholars and those who live in its neighbourhood, are familiar with the three Rembrandts, the Piero di Cosimo, the Watteau, the four Poussins, as well as the three Gainsboroughs at the Dulwich Gallery? Windsor Castle – incredibly – is another example. It is one of the most famous buildings in Europe, yet the paintings and drawings there, by a magnificent collection of masters, are relatively little known. I recall the expression of incredulity by a well informed major American collector on learning how high a proportion of Leornardo drawings are housed there.

The other reason which makes this publication of particular value is the volume of practical information it contains. Most collections, for instance, are growing much faster than their accommodation, and in consequence there are now major works by major artists inevitably relegated to store, to say nothing of many of interest by lesser known figures. Visitors are accordingly given, for instance, guidance as to how to see these unexhibited works, also the times of opening of the various institutions, the means of access by public transport, parking facilities, and even their telephone numbers. A particularly useful feature is a long list of artists, and the collections where their work can be seen.

Also included is a list of the principal commercial galleries and shops which specialise in art books.

Looking through this comprehensively informative book in which more than thirty public institutions are described, one can only wonder why nothing of this kind has been published before.

SIR JOHN ROTHENSTEIN

Introduction

This slim book offers a brief outline of the glorious contents of London's galleries and museums. To keep the book within the limits imposed by price and pocket, it does not deal with sculpture or with the many objects like furniture, clocks, jewellery, pottery and porcelain which we normally think of as applied arts. It deals instead with the thousands of paintings available for public viewing in public and private collections – holdings which make London one of the greatest art centres in the world.

Conventionally, London's visitors – tourists and British residents alike – beat a few well-worn paths to perhaps the National Gallery, the Tate, the British Museum, Hampton Court and Windsor Castle. Part of the purpose of this book is to do homage to these well-worn paths but equally to point out the highways and by-ways which so many people are inclined to miss because they do not know of their existence. For the tourist prepared to look to left and right as well as straight ahead, London is full of rare pleasures to make a visit uniquely rewarding and memorable.

All of us these days have little enough time to do and see all we would wish, so precise information about opening hours and transport and other facilities has been included at the head of each section. To make sure you make no unnecessary journeys, telephone numbers have been included so that you can check on the day of your intended visit that all is well. Opening hours are generous in most cases, but in these days of economic crises and staff shortages, temporary closures have to be anticipated.

A general warning has to be recorded here. Although every effort has been made to ensure that pictures are in a certain place, *all galleries are subject to change and rearrangement without notice*. If your heart is set on seeing a specific work, do telephone in advance and check that it is not in store, on loan, undergoing restoration, or been stolen since this book went to press. If you are particularly interested in the work of an individual artist, you will find the artists' index in Appendix Two (p. 136) will assist you to find out in which specific London collections he or she is represented.

The accounts which follow are fallible and riddled with personal prejudices for I have always thought that a writer who makes his own enthusiasms and dislikes clear, is a truer guide than someone who pretends to a pseudo-objectivity. A prejudice known to the reader can be allowed for, a prejudice cunningly disguised can be insidious.

Accounts of individual rooms assume that the reader is following the unwritten convention that one starts with the works to the left of the entrance and goes around the room clockwise – any departure from this is indicated in the text when it occurs. However, it cannot be stressed enough, *all pictures can be subject to rearrangement and re-hanging elsewhere*. In case of difficulty, do not be afraid to ask the staff on duty – they are normally pleased to make sure that you see what you wish to see. Use this book as a working guide, invest in a comfortable pair of shoes, and, above all, have fun.

Brian Dobbs
London 1975

I
TRAFALGAR SQUARE AND WHITEHALL

The National Gallery

Trafalgar Square WC2. (See map p. 4)
Telephone 01–839–3321
Opening Hours Monday to Saturday 10.00 to 18.00, Sunday 14.00 to 18.00. During the tourist season from June to September the Gallery may continue its experiment of staying open until 21.00 on Tuesdays and Thursdays only.
Closed Christmas Eve, Christmas Day, Boxing Day, New Year's Day and Good Friday.
Admission Free
Parking A commercial car park near at hand but expensive for an extended stay.
How to get there **Mainline Station**: Charing Cross. **Underground**: Trafalgar Square. **Buses**: 1, 1a, 3, 6, 9, 9a, 11, 12, 13, 15, 24, 29, 39, 53, 59, 77, 77a, 77c, 88, 159, 168, 170, 176, 505.
Facilities Restaurant and coffee bar in the basement, reached by stairs in the entrance hall, is open Monday to Saturday 10.00 to 15.00 *and* 15.30 to 17.00, and on Sunday from 14.30 to 17.00. Counters on the ground floor sell postcards, framed and unframed reproductions, black and white and colour prints, and the gallery's own excellent range of publications and catalogues. Free lectures are given at 13.00 Mondays, Wednesdays and Thursdays and at 18.00 on Tuesdays, all from June to September: and during October to May at 13.00 on Mondays, Tuesdays and Wednesdays, and at 12.00 on Saturdays. Check with the gallery to confirm times and subjects.

Two things have to be said about the National Gallery immediately. Firstly, compared with many of the great international collections, it holds a relatively small number of works – though not so small as to grow tiresome in a lifetime of visits; and secondly, the average quality of its canvasses is incredibly high. This is not a collection lifted from mediocrity by a few major works but a living cross-section of the creative heights scaled by Western art up to about 1900. (The Tate holds foreign art of this century, and also the main body of British pictures outside the small but still indispensable selection still held in the National.) To these two formidable arguments for making at least *two* visits to the Gallery, I would like to add a third. It is this.

THE NATIONAL GALLERY

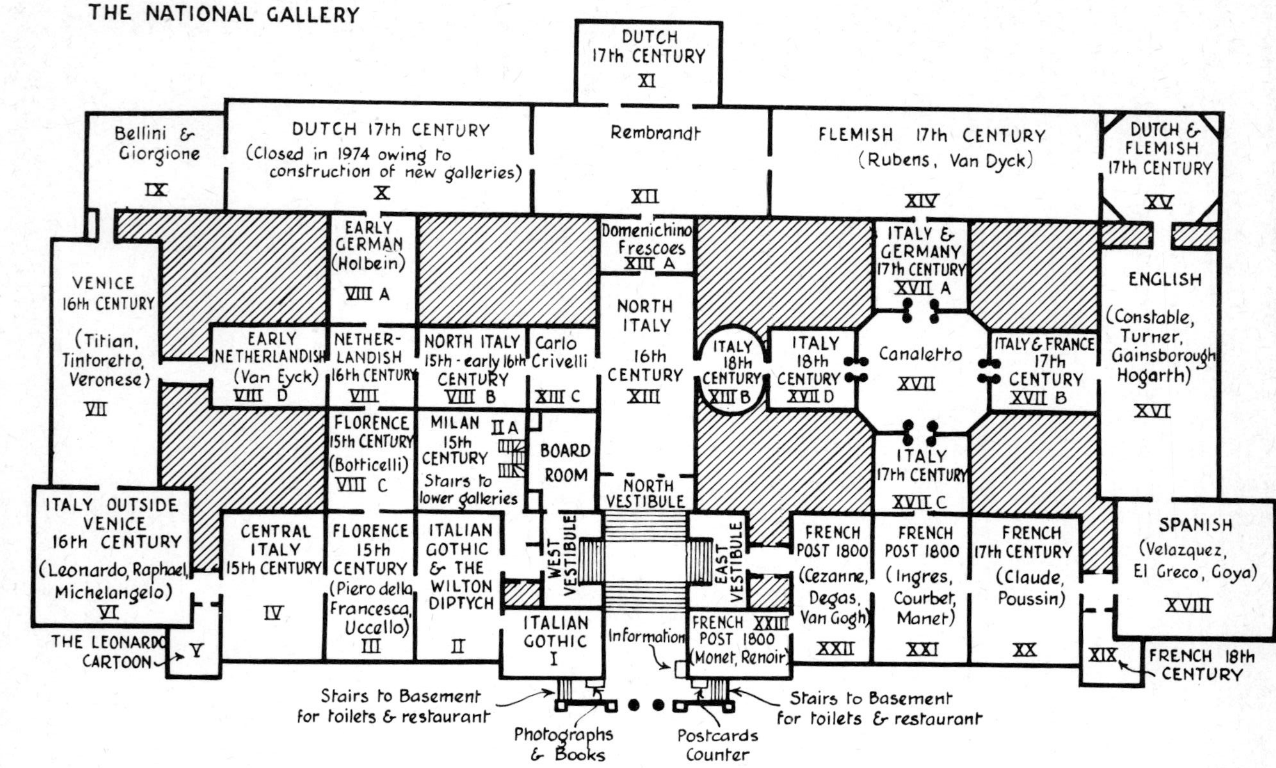

Apart from the obvious necessity of sometimes withdrawing works for cleaning, loan or conservation purposes, and despite the need to rearrange the order of hanging from time to time, the Gallery pursues the enlightened policy of showing somewhere in the building *all* of its holdings *all* of the time, a policy which deserves every plaudit we can give, and a policy some minor and major collections would do well to copy. A word of warning however, before we embark on a room by room tour – two major reshuffles will be taking place in the future, one to coincide with the opening of a new wing (scheduled for about May/June 1975 and which will provide an extra ten rooms* from the present Room X onwards and a new entrance from Orange Street), and another when the air conditioning scheme is completed. *Although maximum care has been taken to ensure accuracy, not all the works may remain in the room indicated in this chapter.* In case of difficulty, the enquiry counter in the vestibule will be glad to assist in the locating of specific works. Also most rooms have a rack of single-page hand guides in which the room's present contents are listed.

On entering the gallery, climb the steps to the first landing (where there is an illuminated floor plan), turn left and go up the next flight too (the West Vestibule). On the right is the Board Room used for special displays and exhibitions of a temporary nature. The next opening on the right leads to Room IIa. IIa features mostly the artists who worked in fifteenth century Milan and who therefore came under the influence of Leonardo da Vinci. Boltraffio, Solario, Foppa and Bergognone all have works in this room. The staircase in the room leads down to eight 'basement' rooms (technically they are on the street level and are therefore the 'ground floor') which contain the entire reserve collection, works which complement the main holdings in the upstairs galleries. I suggest that one makes a tour of the rest of the gallery first, leaving these rooms until last.

Coming out of IIa, turn right and go into Room II, but before getting absorbed in the contents of Room II, turn left into Room I. We are in the world of the Italian Gothic so pause for a moment

* Apart from a central exhibition room, present plans are to allocate the new rooms to Dutch, Flemish, German and Early Netherlandish pictures.

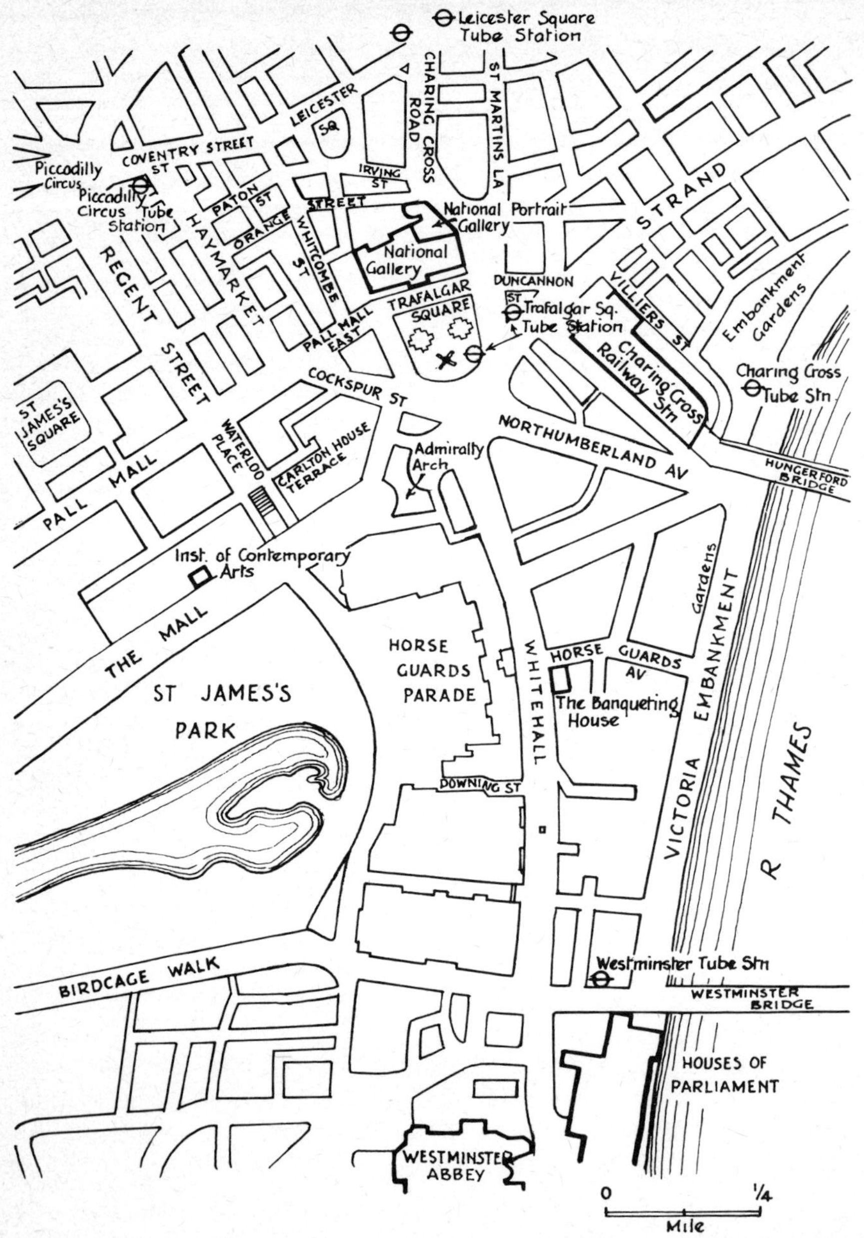

Leicester Square Tube Station
CHARING CROSS ROAD
ST MARTINS LA
LEICESTER
SQ
COVENTRY STREET
Piccadilly Circus
ST
Piccadilly Circus Tube Station
IRVING ST
PATON ST
STREET
ORANGE
HAYMARKET
WHITCOMBE ST
National Portrait Gallery
National Gallery
REGENT STREET
STRAND
DUNCANNON ST
TRAFALGAR SQUARE
Trafalgar Sq. Tube Station
VILLIERS ST
Embankment Gardens
PALL MALL EAST
Charing Cross Railway Stn
Charing Cross Tube Stn
COCKSPUR ST
ST JAMES'S SQUARE
WATERLOO PLACE
CARLTON HOUSE TERRACE
NORTHUMBERLAND AV
Admiralty Arch
HUNGERFORD BRIDGE
PALL MALL
Inst. of Contemporary Arts
Gardens
THE MALL
HORSE GUARDS PARADE
WHITEHALL
HORSE GUARDS AV
VICTORIA EMBANKMENT
ST JAMES'S PARK
The Banqueting House
R THAMES
DOWNING ST
BIRDCAGE WALK
Westminster Tube Stn
WESTMINSTER BRIDGE
HOUSES OF PARLIAMENT
WESTMINSTER ABBEY
0
1/4
Mile

and try to recapture the spirit of a time when every work was a religious one, and every artist painted not for his own glory but for the glory of God. Once dismissed as crude and barbaric, the art of our own times has helped us better to appreciate the compressed yet striking emotional intensity of these works, to say nothing of their more obvious freshness and calligraphic vigour. *Madonna with Child Enthroned* by Margarito of Arezzo is the oldest picture in the whole collection dating from about 1260, more than a hundred years before the *Altarpiece of the Virgin Mary*, Venetian and anonymous. Siena, on the other hand is represented by its greatest son, the masterly Duccio. Here are his small panels *Transfiguration, Annunciation* and *Healing of a Blind Man*, all originally part of his Maestà altarpiece installed in Siena cathedral in June 1311 in a triumphal procession, and which still draws thousands of tourists in the cathedral museum in Siena. Even here the tiny fractions carry some of the impact of the whole. The two *Crucifixes* are by Segna (large) and the Master of San Francesco (small).

Back in Room II and still in the Gothic mould, we can see an altarpiece *Coronation of the Virgin* in the style of Orcagna, seven scenes from the *Life of St Francis* by Sassetta, another altarpiece *Assumption of the Virgin* by Matteo di Giovanni, and, standing on a plinth in the room, half-picture and half-picture-book, the anonymous *Wilton Diptych*. Conceivably owned or commissioned by Richard II from either an English or a French artist (the international gothic *was* international), the book-picture shows the King himself (his emblem was the white hart) being presented to the Virgin and Child, the scene ablaze with gold like an illuminated manuscript. Which, considering that it was painted in about the 1390's, makes it a bit of an anachronism when one remembers that Giotto, the father of Western art had already been dead for about sixty years.

The fifteenth century saw the rapid rise of Florence, financially, politically and artistically. Room II bears some of the fruit including Fra Angelico's *Christ Glorified in the Court of Heaven*, and no less than three superb Piero Della Francesca's – *The Nativity* with angelic carol singers and Joseph sitting right on an ass's saddle; *The Baptism* in which the dove hovering over Christ's head represents the Holy Ghost, and in which the top of His head forms an equilateral triangle with the bottom corners of the picture, a compositional device to emphasise the tranquil gravity of the moment; and *St. Michael*. Also in III is the Masaccio *Virgin and Child Enthroned*, the Masolino *Saints John the Baptist and Jerome*, and the riot of decorative patterning of *Nicolo da Tolentino at the Battle of San Romano* where Uccello shares with us his delight in the new science of perspective (two similar panels are in Florence and Paris). Fra Filippo Lippi, a less than devout monk who eloped with a nun, shows *Seven Saints* and *The Annunciation* (in which the arms of his patrons the Medici family appear under the pot of lilies), Pesellino the *Trinity with Saints*, and Uccello *St George and the Dragon*, colourful, dramatic and historically significant as the earliest picture in the Gallery to be of oil-paint on canvas.

Room IV continues at the same high level with the Umbrian Perugino's *Madonna and Child* altarpiece, the Filippino Lippi (the monk's son) altarpiece *Virgin and Child*, the Pollaiuolo brothers' *Martyrdom of Saint Sebastian* (with the painters as much in love with another new science – anatomy – as was Uccello with perspective), Signorelli's *Virgin and Child* altarpiece and his *The Circumcision* (he incidentally was Della Francesca's pupil), and Piero di Cosimo's *Battle between Centaurs and Lapiths* and his *Mythological Subject*, once thought to be of the death of Procris but now a puzzling enigma awaiting definitive research into Italian myths for solution. On the other hand, Raphael's *Crucifixion* shows pupil outdoing master – his master being Perugino.

At the exit from IV a left turn into the small dim room V brings us to the famous Leonardo *Cartoon*, the subdued lighting preventing fading. Still in Italy, Room VI has moved us on to the sixteenth century. The young Bronzino is represented by his masterpiece *An Allegory of Time and Love*, all brilliant blue drapery and erotic white flesh. Cupid caresses Venus's nipple in more than filial fashion. Father Time (top left) glowers at Truth (top right), Jealousy clutches her own head (left), Pleasure (right) prepares to throw rose petals like confetti and behind him lurks Deceit who proffers a comb of honey in her right hand and a stinged tail in her left, with the added sinister touch that her hands are the wrong ones for the arms. As to the picture's meaning, your guess is as good as mine. Other highlights of the room are Parmigianino's tall altarpiece *Madonna and Child,* Correggio's Ecce *Homo* and *Mercury Instructing Cupid*, Andrea del Sarto's *Young*

Man, and then four works to stop one in one's tracks – two unfinished Michelangelos in *Madonna and Child with St John and Angels*, and *The Entombment*; Raphael's *Ansidei Madonna* with the classically serene Virgin and with St John the Baptist on the left and St Nicholas of Bari on the right (the three balls on the floor right are an emblem for St Nicholas, the original Father Christmas); and then the famous Leonardo *Virgin of the Rocks* (a similar version is in the Louvre) with its strange brooding rocks and enigmatic faces.

With so much yet to see we must move on quickly. VII means Venice and that means the High Renaissance and the great Venetian colourists. The immigrant to Venice from Verona, Paolo Veronese, has a number of works here including *Mary Magdalene laying aside her jewels* (an incident which has no biblical precedent) and the brilliant pageant *The Family of Darius before Alexander*, to say nothing of his puzzling *Allegories of Love*, the four works which hang in the centre of the room. The prolific Tintoretto shows *St George and the Dragon*, and another Veronese, *Adoration of the Kings*, brings us to Titian that other great Venetian who continued to produce masterpieces throughout a life that lasted nearly a century. See *The Holy Family* (a very early work), *The Death of Actaeon* (bought by government, gallery and public subscription for £1¾ million, and which illustrates the legend of Diana turning Actaeon into a stag to be torn to pieces by his own hounds), *Portrait of a Lady, Portrait of a Man* (possibly Titian himself) *Noli me Tangere*, *Bacchus and Ariadne* (cleaned during 1967), and *The Vendramin Family* (once owned by Van Dyck – the story behind the picture is that an Andrea Vendramin dived into a canal to rescue a fragment of the True Cross which remained suspended above the water to allow him to do so – later generations of male Vendramins thereafter prayed to the reliquary to beg the continuation of divine providence to their family). Do not leave the room without also seeing Tintoretto's sensuous and colourful masterpiece *The Origin of the Milky Way*. Here Juno, awakened from her sleep to find herself suckling the illegitimate infant Hercules held by his father Jupiter, pulls away. Drops of her milk fly up to create the stars of the Milky Way, and down to earth to generate the flowers – though a lower part of the work showing the flowers is now lost.

To continue with the Venetian theme, Room IX is mostly devoted to Titian's distinguished predecessor Bellini, though first see the enigmatic Giorgione's *Adoration of the Magi* and *Sunset Landscape with Saints George and Anthony Abbot*. Then let the superb Bellini take you over with *St Dominic*, *Madonna and Child, Agony in the Garden, Blood of the Redeemer, Pièta*, the famous portrait of *Doge Leonardo Loredan* which seems to summarise centuries of Venetian history in one dignified face, *Madonna of the Meadow*, a fine example of religious and landscape imagery combined, and *Assassination of St Peter Martyr* (which should be compared with the version in the Courtauld Galleries (see p. 75) where the tree stumps bleed in sympathy with the victim).

Room X normally devoted to seventeenth century Dutch painting may be closed owing to the work on the new western extension but in any case retrace your steps to Room VII and take the first exit to the left into VIIID, if possible meanwhile adjusting mentally to the differences between Italy and Germany, and between the Mediterranean countries and Northern Europe. How different the ideas and treatments in Early Netherlandish painting can be seen immediately in Gerard David's *Christ Nailed to the Cross* where there is almost an obsession with the blood and cruelty of the scene, coupled with the grim humour of the dog with the skull. And how Hieronymous Bosch's *Christ Crowned With Thorns* and Pieter Bruegel's *Adoration of the Kings* lack any traces of their events being idealised. Rather than call a spade an agricultural implement, one senses that these men would prefer to call it a bleedin' shovel. Note Gerard David's *Canon Bernardus and Saints* and his *Virgin and Child*, the two Rogier van der Weydens – *Pietà* (a very moving image this) and the fragment *Magdalen reading*, and especially the Robert Campin *Virgin and Child with a Firescreen* where the essentially homespun if not ugly mother gives suck to her podgy-cheeked but not entirely healthy child and, as if Campin cannot bear to add so idealised an accessory as a halo, a wickerwork firescreen has to serve instead. The *"Donne" Triptych* by Hans Memlinc was originally commissioned by Sir John Donne, not the poet but a Yorkist supporter in the Wars of the Roses. He and his wife (escorted by St Catherine left and St Barbara right) kneel before Virgin and Child, while the family's patron saints, St John the Baptist (left) and St John the Evangelist (right), occupy the panels in the wings – the background figure in the left-hand wing may be the painter himself. The room's masterpiece, however, is the justly famous Jan van Eyck *The Arnolfini marriage*, signed "Jan van Eyck was here' above the circular mirror, brilliantly coloured, full of exquisite detail and hidden symbolism (the little terrier perhaps represents fidelity, the oranges fruitfulness, the single lit candle in the chandelier the Light of the World, the slippers and sandals the text 'Put off the shoes from thy feet, for the place thou standest is holy ground', and the carved armchair St Margaret, a patroness of married women).

More Netherlandish paintings are in VIII, an octagonal room which can lead into VIIIa, VIIIb, VIIIc and of course VIIId which we have just left. VIII itself has Quinten Massys' *Crucifixion* and *Virgin and Child*, Patenier's *St Jerome* (more landscape than saint), Jan Gossaert's *Little Girl* and also his detailed *Adoration of the Kings*. Germany is represented in VIIIa with Michel Pacher's *Virgin and Child*, Stephen Lochner's *Saints Matthew, Catherine and John*, Hans Baldung's *Portrait of a man*, two Cranachs – *Close of the Silver Age* and *Cupid complaining to Venus* – and Albrecht Altdorfer's *Landscape with Footbridge* which is one of the earliest examples of landscape painted for its own sake. It also has Hans Holbein's *The Ambassadors*, full of objects painted with photographic fidelity – with one exception. Look at the odd elliptical disc at floor level between the men, keep looking at it and move about two paces or six feet to the right of the frame and nearly up to the wall – when you reach the right spot you will see that the object is a distorted perspective skull, presumably an image of death. There are other oddities, the crucifix barely visible extreme top left, the broken string on the lute; it remains a most puzzling picture.

In VIIIb (again reached via VIII), we are back in Italy and the fifteenth century with Francesco Cossa's *St Vincent Ferrer*, Cosimo Tura's *Allegorical Figure* and *Madonna and Child*, Pisanello's *Vision of St Eustace* (if he ever existed Eustace is supposed like St Hubert to have seen a vision of Christ crucified between a stag's antlers), and Mantegna's *Agony in the Garden* and *Madonna and Child* (if Bellini is brought to mind by the wonderful *Agony*, remember that Mantegna was his brother-in-law and a considerable influence upon him).

From VIIIb, go back to VIII and now to VIIIc (with ochre

walls) for fifteenth century Florence and further enigmas at the hands of the half-pagan, half-devout Sandro Botticelli, for example the *Mystic Nativity* (Why do the angels wrestle in the foreground? Why is Mary so tall? Why do the Greek inscriptions evoke the second woe of the Apocalypse from Revelations?). Here also are his *Adoration of the Kings*, his *Portrait of a Young Man*, Filippino Lippi's *Adoration of the Magi*, Baldovinetti's *Portrait of a lady in Yellow*, and another Botticelli puzzle picture in *Venus and Mars* where the warrior has clearly been laid low by love.

Back in VIII for the last time, walk through VIIIb into the small room XIIIc where fifteenth century Venice holds sway in the more than capable form of Carlo Crivelli – look especially at *The Annunciation* where the buildings rival the attendant peacock for colour and ornateness, and the Archangel can hardly get a word in edgeways for the attentions of St Emidius, patron saint of Ascoli, who clearly regards the model of his town more important than the official business in hand; and look also at the *Virgin and Child with Saints Jerome and Sebastian* (otherwise known as the 'Madonna della Rondine' because of the swallow perched high on the throne). Continue into XIII and sixteenth century Italy with Lorenzo Lotto, Moretto, Moroni, Romanino, and Garofalo and then into the small oval room XIIIb for the intimate Italian eighteenth century works by Guardi, Tiepolo and Canaletto. Returning to XIII you may think this is a good time for a coffee, or even to call a halt for the day. If so, the south end of Room XIII leads directly into the North Vestibule with steps back down to the entrance hall where another short flight of steps to the left of the postcard counter leads down to the restaurant. Eyes and feet rested, walk back up the steps into XIII and this time walk straight ahead into XIIIa, a room devoted to Domenichino frescoes based on Ovid's *Metamorphoses* and designed for a villa in Rome. Now is the time also to make another mental adjustment for the next room is XII, and that means Rembrandt. There are other painters represented, but, in the presence of the National Gallery Rembrandts, I always feel diffident about looking elsewhere. How any man can have had the capacity to look at his contemporaries, his loved ones, and even himself with such total honesty, integrity and compassion is beyond my powers to explain. Walk around this room, look at *Saskia in Arcadian costume* (she was his wife, perhaps pregnant here, and she died when she was thirty), *Woman Bathing in a Stream*, *An Elderly Man as Saint Paul*, the dramatically lit *Woman taken in Adultery*, *The Adoration of the Shepherds*, *Belshazzar's Feast*, *An Eighty Year old Woman*, and then at the painter himself in *Self-portrait*, smartly dressed in black, contented, prosperous, and less than forty years old. Then pass on to the *Portrait of the Painter in Old Age* with Rembrandt now crumpled, bulbous-nosed, resigned, poor and an elderly sixty – no flattery, no self-pity but with a massive dignity. Then look at the huge *Equestrian portrait* with its capacity for the flamboyant and public, and contrast it with the intimacy of the twin portraits *Jacob Trip* and *Margaretha Trip* or *An Old Man in an armchair* with the slashing confident brush-strokes on the arm and the strength of the hand – large or small, public or intimate, Rembrandt could paint it, and, as a last glance at the 'Old Age' portrait shows, himself included.

XI can only be reached from the Rembrandt room. Proving seventeenth century Holland had much more than just Rembrandt, it has Hobbema's *Ruins of Brederode Castle* and *The Herring Packers' Tower*, Jacob Van Ruisdael's *Pool surrounded by Trees*, Vermeer's *Lady standing at a Virginal* (and a similar one where the lady sits), de Hoogh's *The Courtyard*, and especially Hobbema's *The Avenue, Middelharnis* inescapably one of the world's most famous pictures. Once back in XII*, Room XIV looms invitingly to the left, where we exchange Dutch intimacy for Flemish grandeur, and for Rubens and Van Dyck in particular. Self-confidence, conviction, and in Rubens' case, unflagging zest and energy, that sometimes threaten almost to break out of the frame, are the keynotes. A group of small Rubens sketches, including one for *A Lion Hunt*, leads us on to *Le Chapeau de Paille* (i.e. The Straw Hat) a ravishing portrait of Ruben's sister-in-law (?) and of which visitors never tire of mentioning that the lady is *not* wearing a straw hat, but scant preparation for the dynamic nudes of *The Brazen Serpent*. It is only something of the size and scope of Van Dyck's equestrian *Charles I* which could stand the competition of Rubens in this room, for fine as Jacob Jordaens' *Double Portrait* is, we soon forget it as Rubens turns his masterly attentions to the landscapes around his home, the

*** If X is open, it will be to your right in which case peruse it now and return to XII before proceeding to XIV.**

Chateau de Steen, in the *Sunset Landscape, The Watering Place*, and *Autumn: the Chateau de Steen*. Trees, skies, water or *The Rape of the Sabines* (in which Rubens' ladies look well capable of holding their own), they all pass beneath Rubens' brush holding no terrors for him. Spare a moment though for the elegant Van Dyck *Abbé Scaglia with the Virgin and Child* before the two Rubens' versions of *The Judgment of Paris*, the later of which has Juno's peacock taking issue with Paris' dog.

From XIV, pass on to the much smaller XV with Nicholas Maes, David Teniers and Jan van Huijsum, and on into XVI with its representative selection of English painting. Turner, arguably our greatest painter, shows why with *Hero and Leander, Ulysses deriding Polyphemus, Rain, Steam and Speed* and *The Fighting Temeraire* amply demonstrating his ability to evoke storm and calm at will and to condense the elements of fire, air and water into paint and canvas. No more powerful a contrast in temperament or approach, though not in talent, can be imagined than between Turner and Reynolds, the original President of the Royal Academy and painter of many portraits similar to *Colonel Tarleton* with the man and his background combined (an approach, Reynolds' detractors claim, that stemmed from his wish to supplement his inability to capture a full likeness by the face and figure alone). Other contrasting approaches to the portrait in England are shown by the infant prodigy Sir Thomas Lawrence in *Queen Charlotte*, by Gainsborough in the formidable *Mrs Siddons*, the charming *The Painter's Daughters*, and the fresh and delightful *The Morning Walk*, an undoubted masterpiece (which incidentally Reynolds thought 'lacked finish'!), and by Hogarth in the sketch-like freedom of *The Shrimp Girl*. Another facet of Hogarth is shown in the *Marriage à la Mode* series of six canvasses. Impossible to discuss fully in a brief space, the story runs roughly as follows; (1) a marriage of financial convenience is arranged; (2) after the marriage, she yawns, he has spent the night elsewhere; (3) the quack doctor prepares to treat the young girl who has caught the husband's venereal disease; (4) the neglected bride now a Countess holds court; (5) the wife's lover caught in the act, so to speak, kills the husband and flees; and (6) the wife commits suicide as her lover has been hanged. Other Gainsboroughs in the room are the early masterpieces *Mr and Mrs Andrews*, and *The Watering Place*. George Stubbs is represented by *Lady and*

Gentleman in a Phaeton and that leads us to Turner's greatest rival Constable, almost the epitome of English landscape and excellently represented here with *The Cornfield* (donated to the gallery by Constable's admirers on his death in 1837), *The Haywain* (which even years of inadequate and hackneyed reproductions cannot diminish in freshness and vigour), and *The Cenotaph*.

From XVI, turn into XVIIb and on into XVII which, like VIII on the western side of the gallery is a central room giving access to a number of others. XVII itself (the dome) has four Venetian scenes, *The Grand Canal, Feast of St Roch, Regatta*, and *Ascension Day*, by Canaletto. Now move into XVIIa and seventeenth century Italy with Guido Reni's vast *Adoration of the Shepherds*, Adam Elsheimer's tiny pictures in the two cases, and the early Caravaggio *Supper at Emmaus* which shows Christ revealing himself to the astonished St Peter and Cleophas (left) as in Luke XXIV verses 30–32. Note that the basket of fruit projects beyond the table-top to add depth to the picture, and that the reason for the very feminine face of Christ may lie in Caravaggio's homosexuality. Back under the dome, go this time to XVIId for eighteenth century Italy and Canaletto's *Venice: a regatta on the Grand Canal*, his excellent *Stone Mason's Yard*, and one of his English excursions *Eton College*. Tiepolo, that most decorative of Venetians, is represented by a number of works including *Vision of St Clement* and the large-scale *Allegory with Venus and Time*. Return to XVII then enter XVIIc for more seventeenth century Italian works by Liss, Carracci, Rosa, Giordano and Solimena. Return to XVII for the last time and enter XVIIb for more seventeenth century pictures, including Claude's *Marriage of Isaac and Rebekah* and *Embarkation of the Queen of Sheba*. Turner much admired these and in accordance with his wishes, two of his own, *Dido building Carthage* and *Sun Rising through Vapour*, hang with them either side of the entrance. The room also shows Dughet, Domenichino, a large and grandiose Salvator Rosa, and a Millet. Exit from XVIIb into XVI and turn right into XVIII.

XVIII holds a marvellous cross-section of about 250 years of Spanish art. Velazquez, one of the world's greatest artists, and one has only to look at the way he handles paint to see why, is represented first in his portraiture – see the full length *Philip IV* and look both at the capturing of the weak features and at the dazzling flicks of paint which trace the embroidered costume, and compare it with the smaller half-length *portrait* of the monarch of nearly thirty years later. In the *Rokeby Venus* (his only surviving nude and the first in the history of Spanish art), on the other hand, Velazquez is trying to out-Titian Titian, not a feat to be lightly undertaken. Another of his portraits is of *Archbishop Fernandes*. Murillo's religious paintings *Two Trinities*, and *Christ at the Pool of Bethesda* – too sweet for some tastes including mine – form a useful standard to judge Velazquez's own religious work in *Christ in the house of Martha and Mary, St John on Patmos*, or *The Immaculate Conception*, where piety is never allowed to swamp reality. Here also is the strange visionary El Greco and his odd almost modern elongations in *Agony in the Garden, Adoration of the name of Jesus*, and *Christ Driving the traders from the Temple*. In a few of his many moods, Goya is here too – as a consummate portraitist with the wide-eyed *Duke of Wellington* (a picture which ironically draws three times the number of visitors it did before it was stolen for a time), *Don Andres del Peral*, and the sultry and beautiful *Dona Isabel de Porcel* – and as a comic satirist with *A Scene from "El Hechizado por Fuerza"*.

From the Spanish room on, the rest of the Gallery is a tribute to the importance of France and her vast contribution to the course of European art. Out of chronological order and easily missed to the left of the exit from XVIII to XX, is the small room XIX with dark blue walls up a short flight of steps. This small selection of pre-Revolutionary France has some small Lancrets, Watteau's *La Gamme d'Amour*, Boucher's *Landscape with Watermill*, Chardin's *The Lesson* and *House of Cards* though it cannot be pretended that here the national collection can rival the glories of the Wallace Collection (see p. 79). Seventeenth century France's two masters Claude and Poussin, both of them spending much of their time in Rome, are the major attractions of Room XX, although Le Nain and Champaigne also creep in. *Aeneas at Delos, Cephalus and Procris*, and *David at the Cave of Adullam*, demonstrate Claude's capacity to people his glowing landscapes with small scale Biblical and classical incidents; while Poussin's figures act out their balletic friezes in the foreground. Poussin's *Bacchanalian Revel, Adoration of the Golden Calf, Cephalus and Aurora, Adoration of the Shepherds*, and *Landscape with a Snake* are all normally in this room.

Room XXI moves us on to the nineteenth century and the conflicts of movements and theories we associate with those exciting times. Here is the *Demoiselles des Bords de la Seine* by the revolutionary Courbet, once a political prisoner, and four paintings by the severe classicist Ingres – *M. de Norvins, Madame Moitessier seated* (a picture which was twelve years in the painting, and one in which the Second Empire interior was for a time supplemented by the sitter's daughter until she was painted out in the latest of Ingres' changes of mind) and the two small antique pictures *Angelica saved by Ruggiero*, and *Oedipus and the Sphinx*. One of Impressionism's earliest contributors, Boudin, has two small *Beach at Trouville* scenes here, and Delacroix, the Romantic antithesis of Ingres' conservative philosophies, has the portrait of *Baron Schwiter* dashed off with all the confidence of a gifted twenty-one year old. On the other hand Degas was in Italy when he was twenty-one and deep in study of the pictorial conventions of the Renaissance – see his *Spartans* here for the results. He was to go on to his more characteristic 'snapshots' of contemporary life later – *La Plage* for example. The brilliant Manet, whose work came to stand as a symbol of revolt against the French academic establishment, and which also caused deep offence for its subject matter, has two works here, *Soldier* and *The Firing Party*, which are fragments of one of his *Execution of Emperor Maximilian* compositions; and two others *La Musique aux Tuileries* and *La Servante de Bocks*. The last two are excellent examples of Manet's ability to show not the generalised truths of myth or religion which had been the stock in trade of European art for centuries, but the immediate truth of the moment – and when the moment is as horrific as the killing of a Mexican emperor, Manet makes *us* into eye-witnesses, and shocks us as a result.

Room XXII is on two levels, take the higher of them first devoted to the man whose painful struggles with form and colour were to wreak the most prodigious of upheavals in methods of painting and methods of seeing alike, and in the process to father most of the trends underlying the art of our own century. I refer of course to Cezanne, seen here with portraits of *The Artist's Father* (an early work) and of his servant *La Vieille au Chapelet*, with landscape *Aix Paysage Rocheux*, and with the huge canvas dominating the room and representing a watershed of modernism – *Les Grandes Baigneuses*, bought for what once seemed a vast £475,000 and now seems an excellent bargain. Stay on this level and pass on into XXIII dominated in the well of the room by Monet's *Water Lilies*, all light and atmosphere and which, on closer inspection, reveals itself to be concave like a theatrical cyclorama. The lower level of this room also has the two Renoirs, *Danseuses*. Return to XXII and descend to the lower level to see Van Gogh's *Sunflowers*, reproductions of which once seemed as ubiquitous an element of bed-sitters as the bed itself, and his *Cornfield and Cypresses*, the desperate late work of a desperate man. Degas' *La La at the Cirque Fernando, Femme Assise*, the pastel *Après le Bain*, and *La Toilette* capture the essence of a fleeting moment, but Seurat's *Baignade* seems more classical, more momentous and lasting – as if painted with the calm of a man in his late sixties. One has to make a conscious effort to remember that the artist had a short, withdrawn life and died at the age of 32. And yet Rousseau, 'Le Douanier' or the Customs Officer, did not even begin to paint until after his fortieth birthday, and then, nagged by his wife, despised by his daughter, and ridiculed by his contemporaries, he produced works of the calibre of the recently acquired *Tropical Storm with Tiger*, the child-like nature of the vision belying the extreme sophistication of the technique. And so we can call a halt to a tour which began many rooms and seven hundred years before and now ends with the work of a humble French civil servant. Do not forget the reserve collection approached from IIa – see p. 3.

For the visitor in a hurry

Although I hope this account of the National Gallery has made it clear that the more skipping one does, the more rare pleasures there are to be missed, it would be a pity to leave someone with but a half hour to spare without some guidance as to what to see. Not in any sense a top sixteen, but a selection of some of the gallery's best known works could be taken in by touring as follows. From the main entrance hall, take the stairs to the left and carry on to Room III to see Piero della Francesca's *Baptism of Christ* and Uccello's *Battle of San Romano*. Carry on through IV and turn left into V to see the Leonardo cartoon. Coming out of V, turn left into VI and see Leonardo's *Madonna of the Rocks*. Take the other exit from VI into VII for Titian's *The Vendramin*

Family and Tintoretto's *Origin of the Milky Way*. From VII turn right into VIIId for Van Eyck's *Arnolfini Marriage*, keep on into VIII and turn left into VIIIa for Holbein's *Ambassadors*. Return to VIII and turn left to walk through VIIIb and XIIIc into XIII. Turn left again and through XIIIa into XII for Rembrandt's *Saskia in Arcadian Costume* (and if you have another 5 minutes to spare, linger in front of the other Rembrandts in this room). Pop in and out of XI for Hobbema's *The Avenue* and turn left again into XIV for Van Dyck's vast *Charles I on horseback*. Go on into XV and out to the right into XVI for Constable's *The Haywain*. Go straight on to XVIII for Velazquez's *Rokeby Venus* and Goya's *Dona Isabel de Porcel*. From XVIII turn right into XX and walk through XX and XXI into XXII for Cezanne's *Les Grandes Baigneuses* on the upper level. Stay on the upper level and go into XXIII for Monet's *Water Lilies*. Return to XXII, descend to the lower level and turn left which leads to the East Vestibule part of the Entrance Hall. Allowing about two minutes for each picture this brief tour should take half an hour and you will have seen enough to make you return another day.

National Portrait Gallery

St Martin's Place, Trafalgar Square WC2. (See map p. 4)
Telephone 01–930–8511
Opening Hours Monday to Friday 10.00 to 17.00, Saturday 10.00 to 18.00, Sunday 14.00 to 18.00
Closed Christmas Eve, Christmas Day, Boxing Day and New Year's Day.
Admission Free
Parking Difficult – private car parks not far away but expensive.
How to get there **Mainline station:** *Charing Cross.* **Underground:** Trafalgar Square, Leicester Square. **Buses:** 1, 3, 6, 9, 11, 12, 13, 14, 15, 19, 22, 24, 29, 53, 59, 77, 88, 159, 170, 176, 506.
Facilities No refreshment facilities but a gallery shop with postcards, books, reproductions and souvenirs. Check with gallery for current details of free lectures.

The National Portrait Gallery is unique amongst London's galleries in that the qualification for a painting's entry to the collection is its subject matter and not its painter or its quality. This can lead

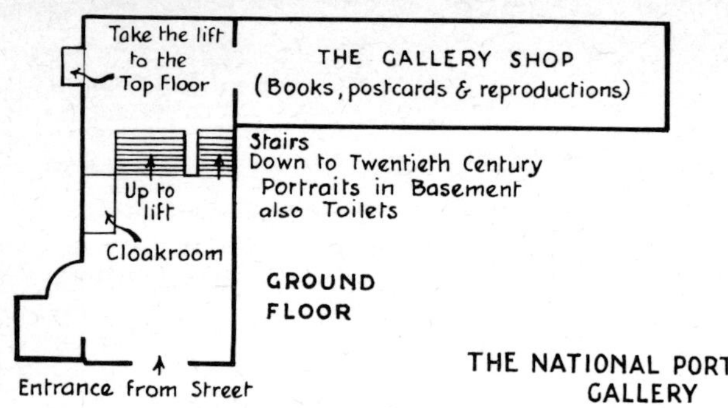

THE NATIONAL PORTRAIT GALLERY

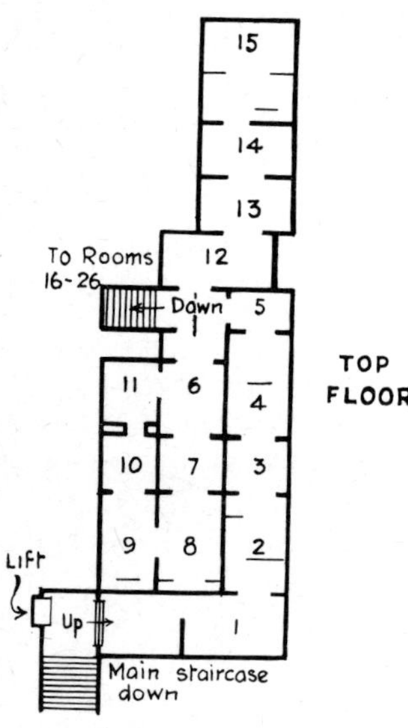

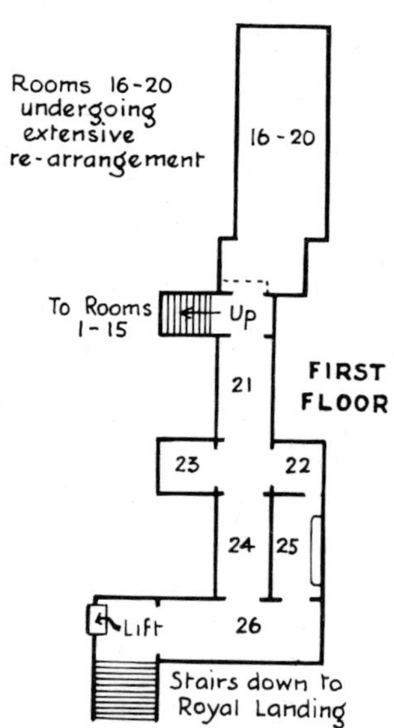

Room 1 THE TUDORS

Rooms 2-5 THE STUART AGE 1603-1714

(2) JAMES I & THE CIVIL WAR

(3) THE ENQUIRING MIND - 17th CENTURY ARTS & SCIENCES

(4) THE RESTORATION & THE CABAL

(5) MARLBOROUGH'S VICTORIES

Room 6-7 THE KIT-CAT CLUB

Room 8 GEORGE I & GEORGE II

Room 9 THE GRAND MANNER - 18th CENTURY ARTS

Room 10 THE EMPIRE

Room 11 GEORGE III

Room 12 ENGLAND AT WAR

Room 13 THE REGENCY

Room 14 THE AGE OF REFORM

Room 15 THE HIGH VICTORIANS

Rooms 21 & 24 (THE CORRIDOR) 19th CENTURY SCIENTISTS, ARTISTS & MEN OF LETTERS

Room 23 19th CENTURY ARTISTS & PATRONS

Room 22 DRAWINGS BY GEORGE RICHMOND etc.

Room 25 THE EDWARDIANS

Room 26 20th CENTURY STATESMEN

to some odd effects with masterpieces cheek by jowl with amateurish daubs rather as if Rembrandt had sent in an entry to the local Townswomen's Guild art show. At its best, however, the gallery offers works where historical importance and technical mastery nicely coincide. The collections and arrangements are liable to change and it is best to make previous arrangements if one specific portrait is what you wish to see.

Once inside the unpromising entrance hall, walk up the stairs to the first landing with Sir James Guthrie's *group portrait* of 1914–18 statesmen and take the lift on the left to the top floor. The gallery is arranged chronologically from the top floor to the basement, and is best viewed in this order.

At the top, outside the lift and on the left is the Chatsworth Cartoon of *Henry VIII* by Hans Holbein the Younger, which closely inspected reveals the pinpricks used to transfer this working drawing on to a wall at the Royal Palace of Whitehall – Palace and mural alike were burnt down in 1698 so this is all that remains of what must have been a striking image. Also on the landing is Michel Sittow's *Henry VII* a version worth comparing with Holbein's more intellectual monarch at his son's shoulder in the cartoon. The Tudor dynasty, which Henry VII founded, and its contemporaries, feature in the room just up the five steps. In the alcove (left) Master John's *Lady Jane Grey* charms in competition with the quaint distorted perspective of *Edward VI* by William Scrots. Also in the room are two portraits of *Elizabeth I*, one by Nicholas Hilliard (probably) and one by Marcus Gheeraerts, an anonymous portrait of *Sir Henry Unton* remarkably combining the man with scenes from his life, and an anonymous painting believed to be of *William Shakespeare*.

Room 2 covers the Jacobean Court which flourished from 1603–1625. On no account miss the *Earl of Arundel* by Sir Peter Paul Rubens opposite the Civil War Display – only a great artist could have caught so well the gleam on the armoured sleeve and the confidence of the upturned eyebrow. Room 3 (with black walls) has Sir Godfrey Kneller's *Dryden* and also his *Sir Isaac Newton* (on the screen) one of his finest works. In the case of miniatures, look for Samuel Cooper's *George Fleetwood*. Room 4 shows *Villiers, Duke of Buckingham* by that one-man painting factory Sir Peter Lely, *Charles II* by Edward Hawker, and John Hayls' well-known *Pepys* (well-known that is for Pepys not for

Hayls). Room 5, patriotically devoted to Marlborough's victories, has a Kneller of *Marlborough trampling the shield of Louis XIV*. Rooms 6 and 7, reached by turning left at the green screen of 'The Hanoverian Succession', are further evidence of the skill of Kneller – no less than 43 portraits of the Kit-Cat Club, the 'Whigs in wigs', a social and literary group that flourished from about 1700–1720 and included Addison, Steele and Vanbrugh. (The club took its name from the mutton pies sold at a Temple Bar public house, and Kneller took his name by anglicising his own – he was originally a German, Gottfried Kniller). Kneller's chief contemporary rival, Michael Dahl, can be seen in the extremely confident and honest *Self Portrait* on the left-hand wall of room 6, while Kneller's own *Self Portrait* is opposite the fireplace.

Room 8 has Jacopo Amigoni's portrait of *Caroline of Anspach* (wife of George II) – the heads peeping out of the cornucopia (and one wonders how so unflattering a symbol was ever thought acceptable) belong to her seven surviving children; and the alcove at the end contains Francis Hayman's *Self Portrait* where artist and sitter are combined. That however is a mere taster for the group of *self-portraits* on the screen to the left of the entrance in Room 9 – Joseph Wright, Johann Zoffany, Allan Ramsay, Angelica Kauffmann, and George Stubbs – quite a collection! particularly when we add those by Gainsborough and Reynolds in the same room. Pausing in Room 10 only for Sir Joshua Reynolds' *Warren Hastings* (with a hint of haughtiness beneath a mild exterior) and in 11 only for his view of *Lord Bute*, we cross the landing with J.S. Copley's *Death of Chatham* on our right and the stairs on our left. Room 12 takes us into Room 13 and the Regency. Here Sir Thomas Lawrence shows up with *Lord Liverpool* (skilful), *Lord Castlereagh* (truthful)) and *George IV* (flatteringly Byronic).

In 14, see Holman Hunt's *Stephen Lushington* and pass on into 15. Rounding the Sir George Hayter *1833 House of Commons,* look to the far wall which has some High Victorian faces on the High Victorian wall-paper. They include G.F. Watts' *Cardinal Manning*, and three by Millais – *Salisbury, Disraeli* and *Gladstone*, showing what brilliant natural talents Millais had. Do not leave without seeing a splendid Ford Madox Brown double portrait of *Henry and Millicent Fawcett* (Fawcett was the blind Liberal

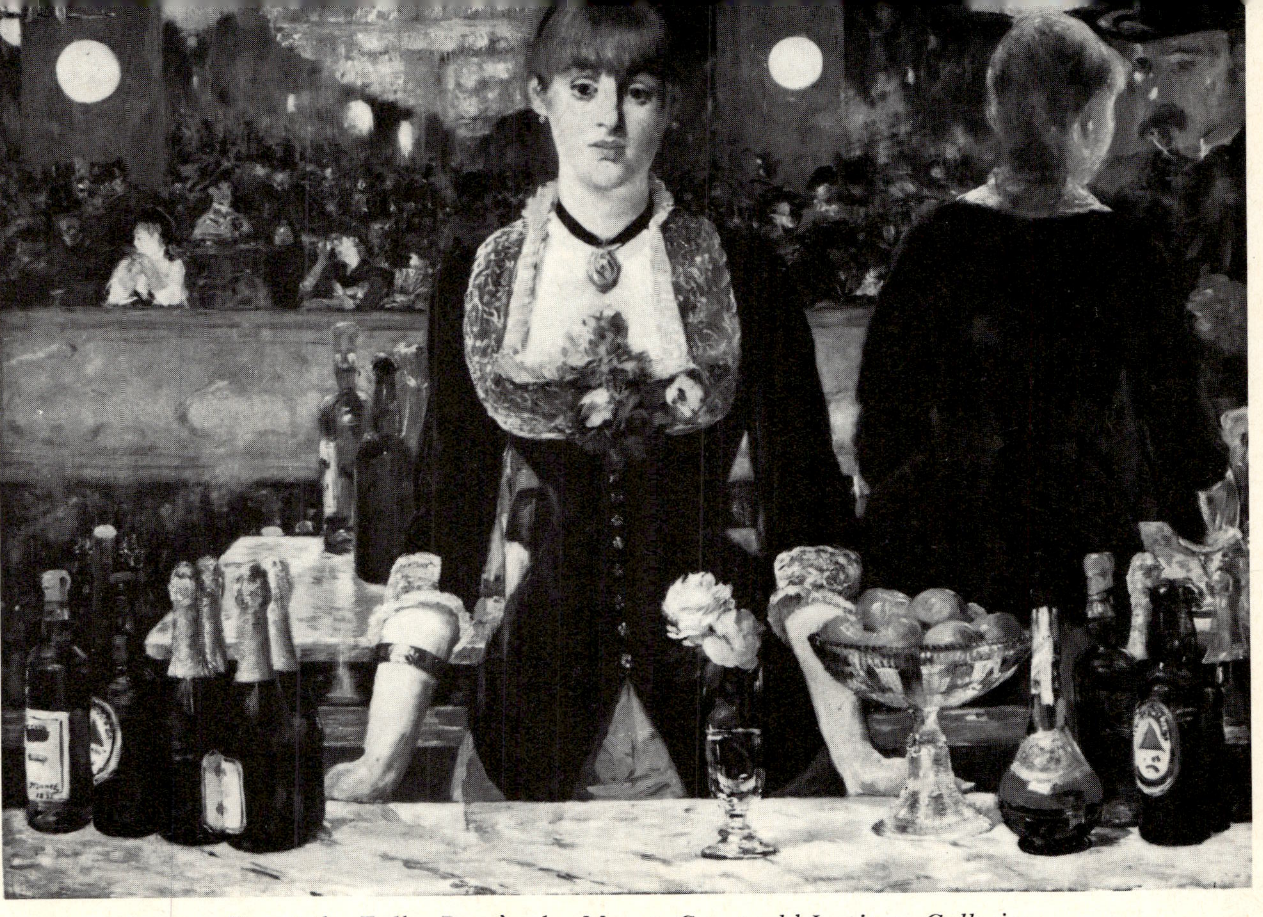

Bar at the Folies-Bergère by Manet, *Courtauld Institute Galleries*

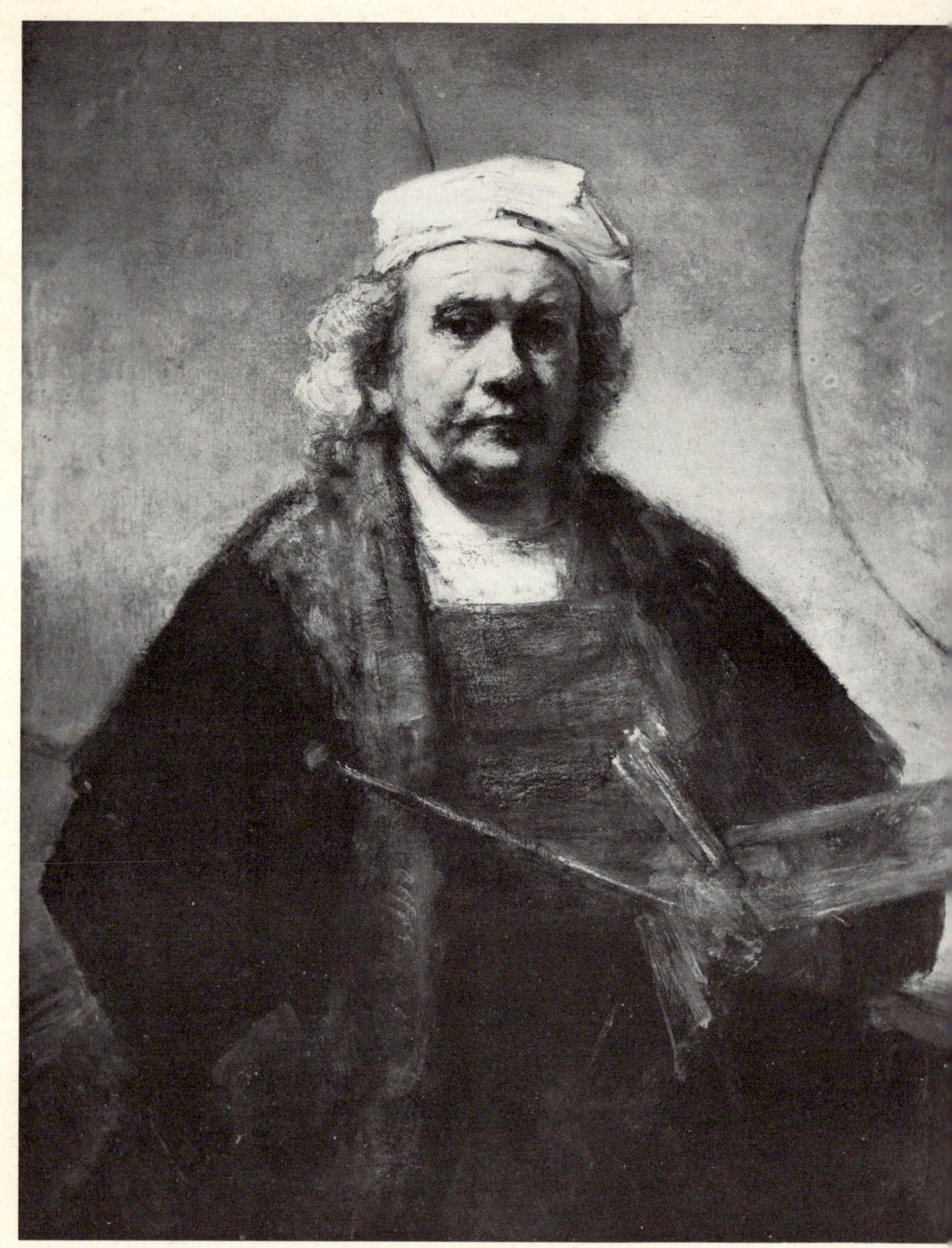

Portrait of the Painter in Old Age by Rembrandt, *Kenwood*

Postmaster General). Retrace your steps to Room 12 and thence back to the landing. The stairs take you down the next floor where rooms 16–20 on the left are being rearranged. To the right, the first half of the corridor itself is 21. Room 22 off the corridor to the left has a host of pastel drawings by George Richmond, and opposite it to the right is 23 with a *Private View of the Royal Avademy 1888*, artists, patrons, socialites and all. The rest of the corridor is 24. Look for G.F. Watts' and George du Maurier's *Self Portraits*, a marvellous evocation of *John Ruskin* by Herkomer, and for a delightful panel of portraits and self-portraits by the young and idealistic Pre-Raphaelites, including three by D.G. Rossetti to show he could draw with the best of them when he put his mind to it. So could G.F. Watts, responsible here for *Matthew Arnold, Tennyson* and *J.S. Mill*. At the end of 24 we are in 26 but turn left and take the doorway in the left hand corner into 25 and 'The Edwardians'. W.B. Richmond's *R.L. Stevenson* was done in one sitting – one hopes he was not paid by the hour. John Singer Sargent's *Henry James* certainly took longer as did his dazzling *Ellen Terry as Lady Macbeth*. Millais' *Arthur Sullivan* is, even here, next to Gilbert but look rather at the William Orpen *New English Art Club*, a sort of pointillist group caricature, and, on the way back to 26, spare a glance for the two drawings of the now-forgotten Charles Conder which include a *Self-portrait*. Room 26 has all the hallmarks of the politician, especially dullness, with even Sickert's *Winston Churchill* doing justice to neither. The stairs at the end lead down to the Royal Landing where things artistic are no better, and in Pietro Annigoni's *Queen Elizabeth II* even worse. Linger by all means in the Gallery Shop, but before leaving do not miss the basement down the stairs from the entrance hall which shows Modernism coming to terms with the academic portrait of the past and succeeding fairly often in amalgamating what might appear to be contradictions. Here are Ceri Richards' *Self-portrait* of 1934, Sir William Orpen's *Augustus John*, Gwen John's *Self-portrait*, Sir Gerald Kelly's *Somerset Maugham* (a glossy debonair image of the young man about town which contrasts powerfully with the lived-in face of the writer in Graham Sutherland's famous portrait in the Tate), Patrick Heron's *T.S. Eliot*, Nina Hamnett's curious and charming *Lytton Strachey*, Vanessa Bell's *Leonard Woolf* (I could do without the sentimental dog), William Roberts' group *The Vorticists*, David Bomberg's pencil *Self-portrait*, and another *Self-portrait* by John Minton, the young English artist who died tragically in 1957. (If the camera appeals to you as much as the brush, do not forget that the Gallery has opened an extension at 15 Carlton House Terrace – see map p. 4).

Institute of Contemporary Arts (ICA) ✓

Nash House, The Mall, S.W.1. (See map p. 4)
Telephone (Gallery and offices only) 01–839–5344
Open to non-members for special temporary exhibitions only. See daily newspapers for opening hours and exhibition details.
Admission charge Refreshment facilities when open.
Parking probably a capital offence
How to get there As for the National Gallery (see p. 1) – no buses go down the Mall.

Rarely did so austere an exterior – all part of Nash's Regency elegance – conceal such an artistic *enfant terrible* as the ICA galleries in the Mall. Perhaps a very mild *enfant* by the standards of East coast and West coast American happenings and non-happenings; it has nevertheless housed in its time, experimental offerings in theatre, cinema, computer art, kinetic art, illusory art and the like, all revolutionary by London standards. It has its place here as an avant-garde outpost in an area of museum art, and as such, one should keep it in mind when on a visit to the vicinity.

The Banqueting House

Whitehall, S.W.1. Situated at the junction of Whitehall and Horseguards Avenue. (See map p. 4)
Telephone 01–930–4179
Opening Hours Monday to Saturday 10.00 to 17.00; Sunday 14.00 to 17.00
Closed Good Friday, Christmas Day, Boxing Day and New Year's Day.
Small admission charge
Parking Difficult
How to get there **Mainline station**: Charing Cross. **Underground**: Charing Cross, Westminster, Trafalgar Square. **Buses**: 3, 11, 12, 24,

29, 39, 53, 59, 76, 77, 77a, 77c, 88, 159, 168, 170.

For a building so full of historic and artistic significance, the Banqueting House has the most discreet if not anonymous entrance of any I know. If, walking along the eastern pavement of Whitehall, one were to blink at an inappropriate moment, one might miss completely the Palladian building that saw the Stuart family at its zenith and at its nadir. It was here in this building, built of Portland stone by Inigo Jones at the behest of James I, that Charles I, a monarch of much aesthetic sensibility, engaged the great Rubens to do homage to James' memory in a series of nine allegorical ceiling paintings. Rubens graced the vacant panels of Jones' ceiling with masterpieces that are still one of the greatest glories of the Royal collection, and got £3,000 and a knighthood in return. However, his royal patron's reflected glory was not to last, for, on a bitter cold January afternoon in 1649, Charles himself passed beneath Rubens' depiction of the triumph of wisdom and justice over rebellion and falsehood, to lay his head on a black-draped block a few yards away, and to 'be put to death by severing of his head from his Body'. Eleven years later in 1660 both Houses of Parliament gathered here to welcome home the restored Charles II who was to give an annual demonstration of the temporary change in Stuart fortunes by laying his hands on scrofulous patients brought before him, thus curing them of the disease known as the 'King's Evil'. The Stuart fortunes did not last and the room's final contribution to the pageantry of English history was to provide the setting for the formal acceptance of the crown of England by William and Mary in 1689.

I give this historical preamble to enable the visitor to recapture some of the eloquent grandeur that Rubens evokes in his ceiling paintings. From the entrance hall counter, walk up the short flight of stairs with a passing nod to the portrait of *Charles II* by J. Michael Wright painted around the time of the Restoration, then pause at the double doors leading to the Banqueting Hall proper as many a seventeenth century ambassador must have paused before you. (Rubens himself was sometimes sent on diplomatic errands).

The eye travels not so much to the red canopy and the chair thrones at the far end of the room, but rather up to the gorgeous ceiling panels, delicately yet flamboyantly delineated by gold and white decorated borders, and shown to their best advantage by the creamy-white and pilastered interior.

From where you stand, the great oval panel represents the *Apotheosis of James I*, a turbulent and dynamic composition amply demonstrating a baroque ability to flatter a monarch or patron unblushingly, and Rubens' capacity to give fleshy reality to abstract ideas. Similarly, the long rectangular panels to either side of the central oval show some exceedingly well-fed cherubs bearing off the many fruits of Stuart rule. In the oval itself, James is at the base, the muscular lady on the right with book and scales is, at a guess, Justice, and the one on the left with an urn, Religious Truth. The airborne angels and cherubs above the royal head bear a hero's crown of laurel and also Mercury's magic wand, the Caduceus (Mercury was the Divine Herald conventionally attending on Last Journeys).

As you advance into the centre of the room, the painting above the throne can be seen – *The Benefits of the Government of James I.* James is in the centre; two cherubs swoop down with a laurel crown; Minerva (i.e. the protector of civilised life) sees off Mars (who carries a flaming torch of War) to the right; while to the left, Peace embraces the sitting Plenty. In the ovals to the sides are (*left*) Reason triumphing over Intemperate Discord and (*right*) Abundance bestriding Greed.

Now turn around to get a throne's eye view of the paintings above the entrance. The central panel, with James perched Solomon-like on the throne to the right, shows the symbolic *Union of England and Scotland*, the newly-born union itself represented by the naked child escorted by 'England' and 'Scotland' both baring a breast for the occasion, and Britannia about to crown him with double crowns. Above them all, the cherubs carry the emblem of the new United Kingdom in case we have still failed to get the point. The ovals to the side are this time (*left*) a strapping Hercules taking a club to Envy (or perhaps Scottish rebellion?) and (*right*) Wisdom (Minerva) taking a spear to Ignorance.

It is not the significance of the subject matter, these painted hymns of praise to a dynasty long gone, that now appeals to us however (though the works might baffle without some notes on their subjects). It is rather the evidence before us of a great painter in full possession of his stupendous and Olympian powers – he painted them in about 1630 and died in 1640 – proof if any were needed that Sir Peter Paul Rubens was indeed the Prince of Painters.

2
MILLBANK

The Tate Gallery ✓

Millbank, S.W.1 (See map p. 30)
Telephone 01–828–1212 (Publications 01–828–8383 or 01–834–5651: Restaurant 01–834–6754)
Opening Hours Monday to Saturday 10.00 to 18.00 (extended to 20.00 on Tuesdays and Thursdays only): Sunday (including Easter Sunday) 14.00 to 18.00.
Closed Good Friday, Christmas Eve, Christmas Day, Boxing Day, and New Year's Day.
Admission Free.
Parking Four hour parking meters in the vicinity of the gallery if you are lucky.
How to get there **Underground**: Pimlico (also Westminster about ¾ mile away), **Buses**: 77 and 88 stop at the gallery, 2, 36, and 185 in the vicinity.
Facilities Restaurant (moderately expensive but good) in basement – open 12.00 to 15.00 Monday to Saturday, *Closed Sundays*. Coffee shop (and self-service snacks) in basement – open Monday to Saturday 10.30 to 17.30 *and* Sunday 14.00 to 17.30. Gallery shop (with postcards, reproductions – framed and unframed, and books) on left of entrance hall, open 10.00 to 17.30 Monday to Saturday, and Sunday 14.00 to 17.00. Information desk in entrance hall. Free daytime and evening lectures and films held regularly at the gallery – check with the education department for details. Special arrangements are willingly provided for the disabled – call at the Atterbury Street entrance where a ramp and lift are provided for wheelchairs, and also where free wheelchairs are provided if required. The gallery also runs a Friends of the Tate society, membership of which gives access to private views, to a private room at the gallery, to the reference library and free admission to special Tate exhibitions – apply by post to the Organising Secretary, Friends of the Tate at the gallery, or telephone 01–834–2742 or 01–828–1212.

The Tate has three main functions. It houses the national collection of British paintings (except for the select holdings at the National Gallery – see p. 12), it holds the national collection of modern foreign paintings (taking over, broadly speaking, where the National Gallery chronologically leaves off). It also stages

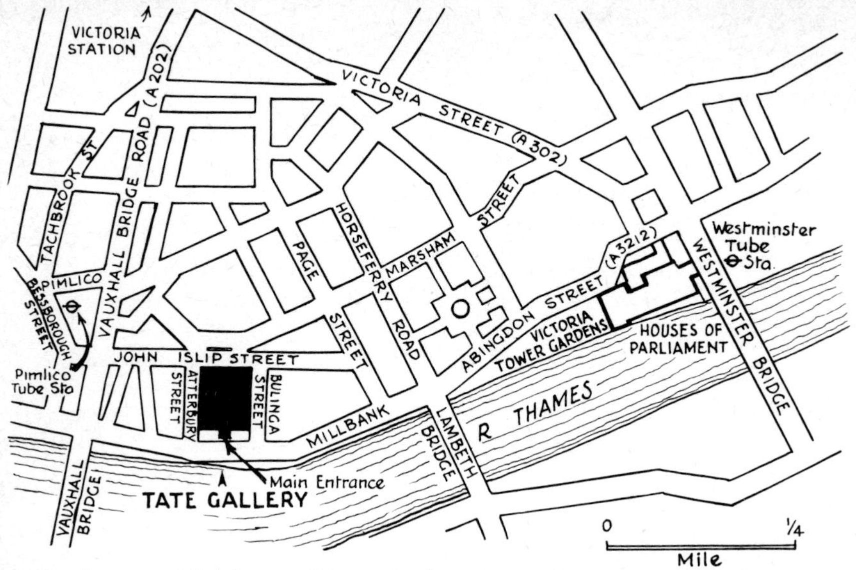

major loan exhibitions of international standing.

Unfortunately, it has space only to show about one quarter of its collection at any one time and therefore changes the paintings on exhibition more frequently than most – to see any specific work, it is best to contact the gallery well in advance if disappointment is to be avoided. Again every effort has been made to ensure the accuracy of this chapter, but *the exact location of specific works cannot be guaranteed.* In fact, on one memorable occasion, I saw one of the Tate's own lecturers, a sheaf of notes under his arm and all prepared to discuss a specific canvas for the benefit of a large and eager audience, stopped in his tracks by the realisation that the canvas had been taken away that very morning!

Once inside the central hall next to the coats and bags counter, stand with your back to the main entrance. You are now facing the sculpture hall and special exhibition area. To your right, half the gallery carries the modern foreign works. To your left, the other half of the gallery accommodates the British collection. It is there we start with Room 3 (next door to the Gallery Shop).

All the giants of English eighteenth century painting are here, with one exception. Three Stubbs studies whet our appetite for the recently acquired *Hound and Bitch* by the same artist, an artist of genius employed to record for posterity a rich man's favourite

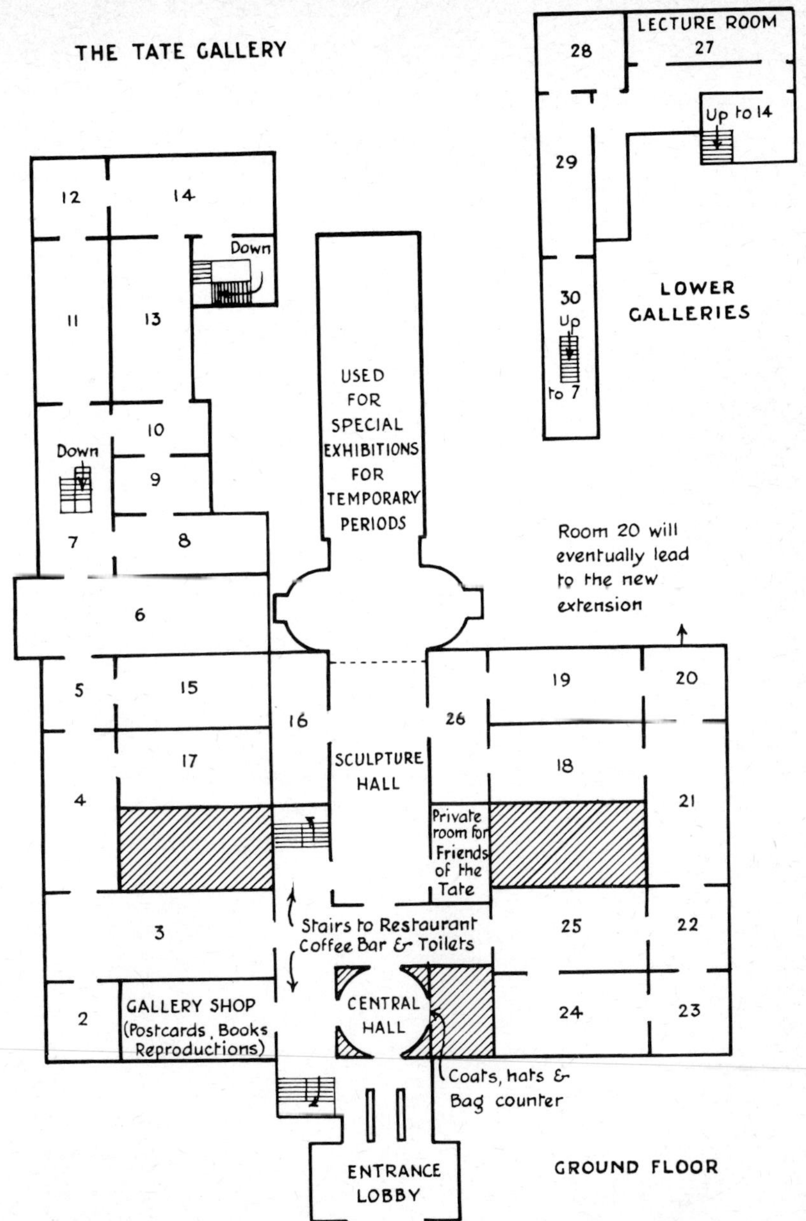
THE TATE GALLERY
LECTURE ROOM
27
28
Up to 14
29
30
Up
to 7
LOWER
GALLERIES
12
14
Down
11
13
10
Down
9
7
8
6
USED
FOR
SPECIAL
EXHIBITIONS
FOR
TEMPORARY
PERIODS
Room 20 will
eventually lead
to the new
extension
5
15
16
26
19
20
17
SCULPTURE
HALL
18
4
21
Private
room for
Friends
of the
Tate
3
Stairs to Restaurant
Coffee Bar & Toilets
25
22
2
GALLERY SHOP
(Postcards, Books
Reproductions)
CENTRAL
HALL
24
23
Coats, hats &
Bag counter
ENTRANCE
LOBBY
GROUND FLOOR

pets. If it were not ungallant, one could say the same for Zoffany's portrait of *Mrs Catherine Wodhull.* Stubbs' mastery of equine proportions can be seen in *Mares and Foals*, interesting to compare with Reynolds' *Lord Ligonier* where the horse is part of the background rather than the subject. Gainsborough is represented by the portrait of *Mr and Mrs John Joshua Kirby*, by the *View of Dedham* (an excellent landscape) and by a number of others including *Mary* (his daughter) and a glass case of prints showing his copperplate techniques. A rival landscape artist Richard Wilson, whose best work is in private hands, has a number of works here too.

The exception I mentioned is in Room 2, reached only from 3. He is William Hogarth, shown here in a number of his roles; social commentator, portraitist, satirist, and grand mannerist among them. Here are *Southwark Fair, The Beggar's Opera* (John Gay's comic opera, a subject to which Hogarth was to return a number of times), *Dr Hoadley* (here in his Chancellor of the Garter robes, he was Bishop of Westminster), *Satan, Sin and Death* (based on Milton's *Paradise Lost* Book II), *Self-portrait with Pug* (the dog was his beloved Trump), *Roast Beef of Old England* (a scene at the Calais Gate designed as a xenophobic attack on all things French, Hogarth sketching in the corner), *The Graham Children* (all disturbingly like little adults) and *The Artist's Servants* (painted to accompany Hogarth's old age).

From 2, cross 3 and walk into 4 opposite. Here Reynolds is by turn stern (*Admiral Keppel*), sweet (*Age of Innocence*) and analytical (three *self-portraits* at various ages). Zoffany's *The Bradshaw family*, Joseph Wright's *Experiment with the air-pump* (which looks splendidly like a Caravaggio transplanted to the English industrial revolution) and his *Sir Brooke Boothby* are all here, and on the screen is John S. Copley's *Death of Major Pierson*, a large, colourful and dramatic example of the art of history painting. Also here are James Barry's large and neo-classical *King Lear weeping over Cordelia* and Angelica Kaufmann's fine *Self-portrait.* To the right off 4 is 17, a room at present given over to Andy Warhol, whether in recognition of his gifts as an artist or his skill as a publicist I would not care to say. Behind the Copley screen is *John Philip Kemble as Hamlet* by Lawrence and also the entrance to Room 5 devoted to the strange Fuseli and the spectacular de Loutherbourg. Fuseli's *The*

Shepherd's Dream (from *Paradise Lost*), and *Lady Macbeth seizing the daggers* are imaginative and flamboyant enough, but look for a time at *Titania and Bottom* – conventional at first glance, but then the curious details take over, the coy lady on the right with a little old man on a lead, and the malevolent yellow-eyed gnome in the right hand lower corner, for example. De Loutherbourg was Garrick's scenery and lighting expert at the Drury Lane theatre, and his interest in special effects can be seen in *Battle of Camperdown*, *Battle of the Nile*, and especially in *Avalanche in the Alps*. To the right off 5 is Room 15 with a selection of excellent modern works including Peter Blake's charming *On the Balcony, The Fine Art Bit, Toy Shop* (a full reconstruction of a tiny shop facade), and *The Masked Zebra Kid* all in the Pop idiom; David Hockney's *The First Marriage*, Roy Lichtenstein's *Whaam!* (the comic-strip writ large and a controversial purchase in 1966), a relatively dull Robert Rauschenberg in *Almanac,* and Tom Phillips' dazzling *Benches*.

Rooms 6 to 10 are devoted to a magnificent display of Turners, a supreme accolade to a supreme painter. With the light pleasantly diffused by overhead muslin, Room 6 itself is divided into three sections. The first with *Fishermen at sea off the Needles, Fall of an Avalanche,* and *Snowstorm: Hannibal crossing the Alps* is Turner, the admirer of Claude and Poussin. The second is the Turner developing English landscape and rivalling Constable – look at *London from Greenwich* for the way the painter captures the feeling of the light after a storm. The third is the Turner never seen in his own lifetime – works done at Petworth House and on the Isle of Wight, where pictorial conventions have been challenged, found wanting and unhesitatingly discarded – *Dinner in a Great Room, A Vaulted Hall, The Thames from Above Waterloo Bridge, Music Party, Petworth* and *Shipping with a Flag*. Room 7 is Turner post 1830, the later works including *Yacht Approaching the Coast, Norham Castle, sunrise, A Fire at Sea, Peace: Burial at Sea, Venice: the Piazzetta with the Doge marrying the sea, Sun Setting over a Lake, The Angel Standing in the Sun, Breakers on a Flat Beach,* and *Snow Storm: Steam Boat off a Harbour mouth* (for which Turner tied himself to the mast to study the phenomenon at first hand); all of them mature masterpieces and dazzling in their technique and grandeur of conception alike. (Room 7 has a flight of stairs leading to the lower galleries, but another access point will present itself later). Room 8 to the right has *Palestrina, Regulus,* and *Vision of Medea* (a novel solution to a framing problem that any do-it-yourself expert might envy). Room 9 has some small studies, and the fascinating pair, *Shade and Darkness* and *Light and Colour (Goethe's theory)* – the latter a circular vortex of pale yellow light. Room 10 contains experimental watercolours and an oil *Self-portrait*.

Room 10 leads you back into 7, then turn right into Room 11 which had red ochre walls and bays. Here a group of small works by Turner's rival Constable leads to *Flatford Mill*, and a number of his oil sketches of Hampstead Heath leads to *The Glebe Farm*. Other early nineteenth century painters are also here – John Martin, the Cecil B. De Mille of his day, with his apocalyptic *The Great Day of His Wrath,* John Crome in the quieter vein of *Slate Quarries*, Francis Danby with the vast *The Deluge*, its clever lighting perhaps best seen from about twenty feet away, and a group of small Boningtons, and then some more Constables including *Chain Pier, Brighton* and a lively sketch *Hadleigh Castle*. Totally dominating the room though is James Ward's scowling *Gordale Scar,* Yorkshire redrawn to epic proportions.

Behind it is Room 12, not to all tastes, but, if one can bear with Victorian canvasses aspiring to the novel, of great interest. For the student prepared to consider the unfashionable or sentimental on its own terms, this is one of the most rewarding rooms there is. If I seem to proselytise unduly, that is because the works are all too often rejected or ridiculed virtually unseen. William Mulready's *The Last In*, Atkinson Grimshaw's *Liverpool Quay* (Grimshaw specialised in nocturnal moonlight effects like this very successful canvas), Augustus Egg's *Past and Present 1, 2, and 3* (1. shows an adulterous wife who has betrayed her husband and children. 2. and 3. show the same moon shining on the now destitute adultress and on her betrayed family), William Frith's famous *Derby Day* (an anecdotal sociologist's delight), R.B. Martineau's *Last Day in the Old Home* (ten years in the painting, with the racing print in the bottom left and the form book in the man's hand telling us very clearly *why* the happy home is being sold), Henry Wallis' *Death of Chatterton* (for which novelist George Meredith was the model), Edward Burne-Jones' *King Cophetua and the Beggar Maid*, and the French refugee from the Franco-Prussian war James

Tissot's *The Ball on Shipboard*.

Room 14 continues in Victorian vein with John William Waterhouse's *Lady of Shalott*, a G.F. Watts *Self-portrait*, and a wall of Sargents including the aristocratic *Lord Ribblesdale* after which Henry Herbert la Thangue's crass *Man with a Scythe* is a descent to banality, whereas Luke Fildes' *The Doctor* was at least an attempt at useful social propaganda. 14 has a narrow entrance to 13 with Walter Greaves' semi-primitive and charming *Hammersmith Bridge on Boat Race Day*, Walter Sickert's *Sir Alec Martin* and *Lady Martin*, and his devastating comment on the English Sunday, *L'Ennui*. In this room too can sometimes be found some of the Tate Whistlers including *Old Battersea Bridge* and *The Little White Girl*. Return to 14 and take the exit to the right to the staircase to the lower galleries. At the top of the stairs are two striking Stanley Spencers, *Resurrection* of 1950 and another of 1926, symptomatic of this English visionary who stayed in his Thames-side village, Cookham, and used it as a background for hundreds of works of a Christian nature. Alongside the stairs are his *Self-portrait* (aged 21), *Daphne, Swan Upping at Cookham*, and *St Francis and the Birds*. At the foot of the stairs is a small group of Henry Moore drawings, Alfred Wallis seascapes and Ben Nicholsons, leading to the corridor alongside the lecture theatre. In the corridor are a number of Victor Pasmores – *Nude* and *Thames at Chiswick* in his early naturalistic style, and *Square Motif* in his later abstract mode. Also here are John Piper's *Seaton Delaval*, a group of Graham Sutherlands including *Somerset Maugham* (to be contrasted with the one by Gerald Kelly in the National Portrait Gallery).

To the right off the corridor is Room 28 devoted to the Pre-Raphaelites, not quite rivalling Manchester or Liverpool, but easily the best anywhere in the capital. The young men's mid-century protest against the materialism around them and against prevailing academic presumptions is here represented by Ford Madox Brown's *Chaucer at the Court of Edward III* and *Jesus washing Peter's Feet*, William Morris' *Queen Guinevere* (probably Morris' only picture), Dante Gabriel Rossetti's *Girlhood of Mary, The Annunciation, The Beloved* (taken from the Song of Solomon), *Proserpine* and *Beata Beatrix*, John Everett Millais's *Christ in the Carpenter's Shop* (once subject to a bitter attack by Dickens) and *Ophelia* to show how precociously he was talented, and *The Order of Release of 1746* to show how sentimental he became later on his way to the Presidency of the Royal Academy, Arthur Hughes' *April Love*, and a version of Ford Madox Brown's *The Last of England*. Taking the alternative exit to Room 28 takes us into 29. Look at the beautifully controlled light in William Dyce's *Pegwell Bay*, and at the left-hand wall with its group of Samuel Palmers, including *Coming From Evening Church*, and *A Hilly Scene*, not forgetting some Blake-like George Richmonds including *Abel the Shepherd*. Now walk to the doorway at the far end of the room for from here we can follow the chronological development of one of England's great visionaries, mystic and genius William Blake. His early works, interesting if crude, lead on to the large colour prints of 1795, arguably his greatest achievement and including *Elohim creating Adam* (seemingly rejecting the orthodox Biblical account), *The House of Death, Newton* (scornfully depicted as a slave to reason), *Nebuchadnezzar* (scornfully depicted as a slave to animal senses) and *Pity* (with its streaming horses and the tender fingers of the rider supporting the baby). The tempera works of 1799–1800 turn to biblical subjects as do the watercolours of 1800–5 – these were all commissioned works and vary from delicate to dramatic. Blake's total failure in his exhibition of 1809 led to a long period of obscurity. The sombre oils from the exhibition include *The Spiritual Form of Pitt guiding Behemoth* (which Blake himself would have liked to paint a hundred feet high), and *The Spiritual Form of Nelson guiding Leviathan*. In the works of the 1820's, note *The Body of Abel Found by Adam and Eve* and then look at the series of illustrations for Dante's Inferno (on the wall opposite the works by Samuel Palmer). These masterly and glowing water-colours were carried out in the closing years of Blake's life, the last offerings of a unique genius. Leave the Blake room at the entrance next to his early works and you are in 30 which has watercolours by Cozens, Girtin and Edward Lear. Go up the staircase, turn around at the top of the stairs, and you are back in Room 7. Go back through 6,5,4 and once in 3, turn left and walk out into the narrow corridor. It has a staircase leading down to the coffee bar and restaurant, this being a very convenient place for a rest before continuing with our exploration of the second half of the Tate.

This second half, devoted to modern foreign and British painting, is more prone to change than any part of the collection,

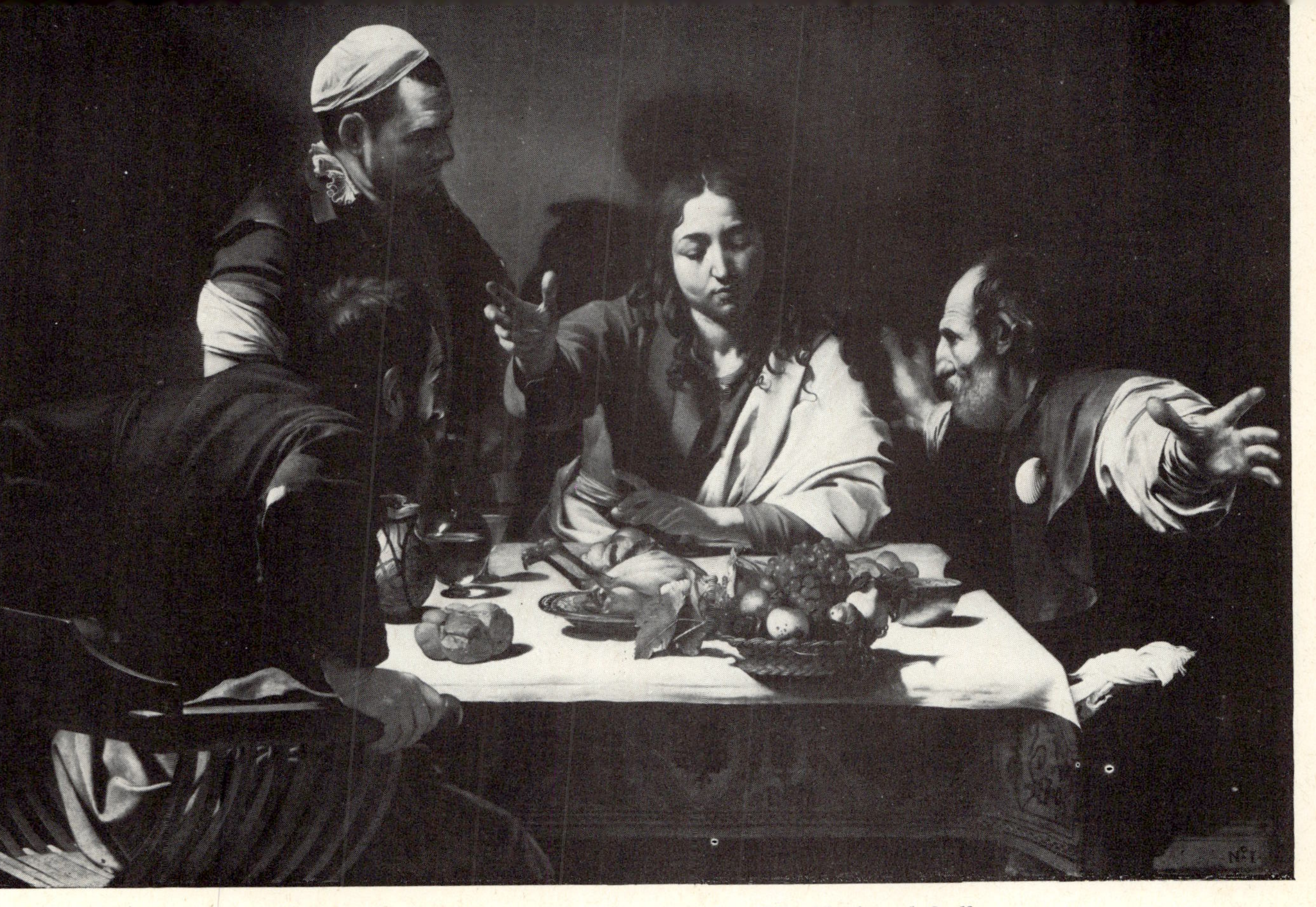

The Supper at Emmaus by Caravaggio, *The National Gallery*

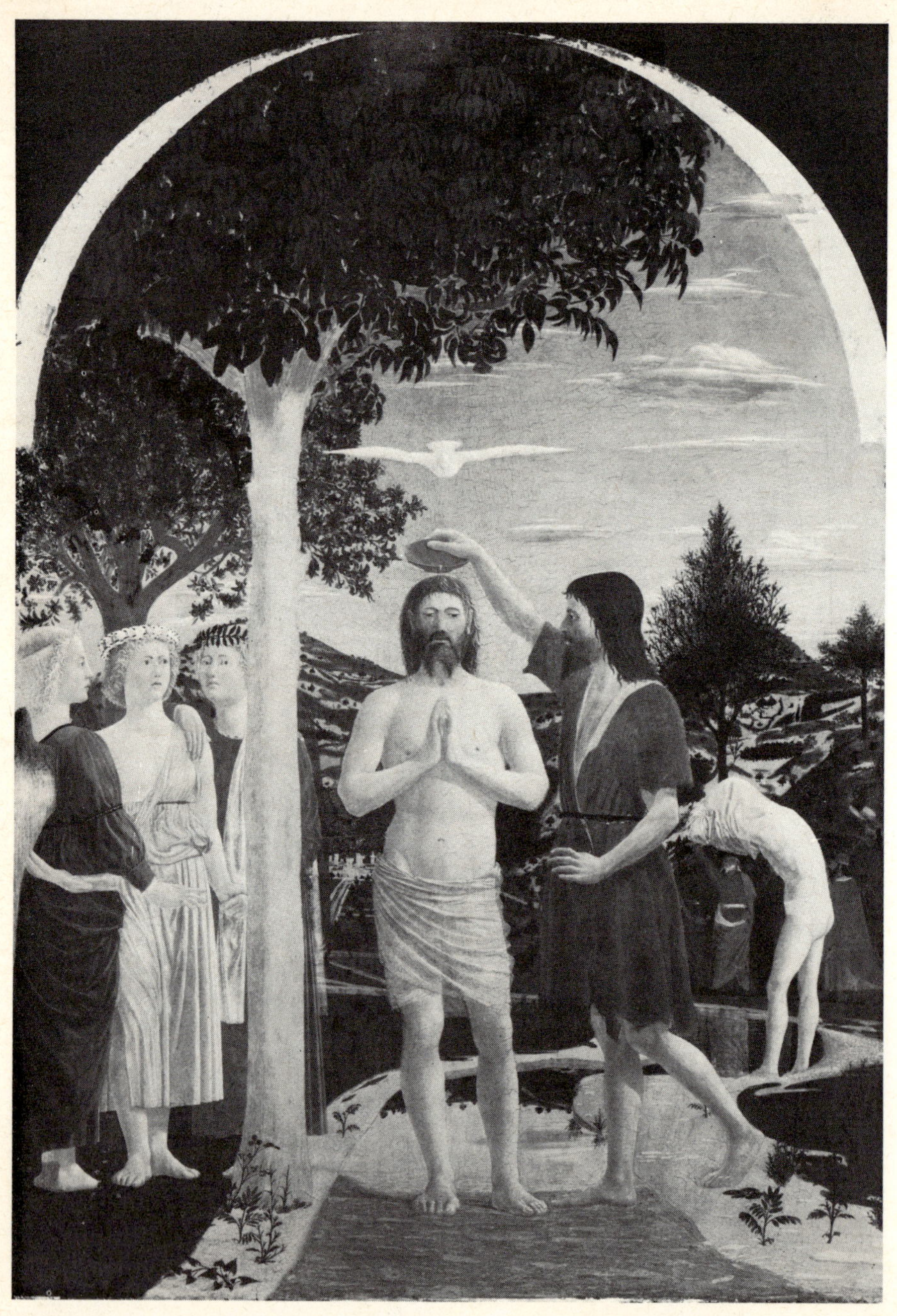

The Baptism of Christ by Piero della Francesca, *The National Gallery*

so much so that it would be foolish to attempt a room to room guide. Suffice it to say that all the major schools and trends of the last seventy years are represented – Impressionism, the Post-Impressionists, the Fauves, the Futurists, the Cubists, the Constructivists, the Expressionists, the Surrealists, the Vorticists, the Dadaists, the Formal Abstractionists, the Abstract Expressionists, the Op and Kinetic Artists, and the Pop Artists included. Start at Room 25 to the right of the central hall (where we began originally) and follow the rooms through (see the ground plan p.31). Room 20 will eventually lead to a new extension expected for March/April 1976 which will give 50% more space in a new adjustable area. Room 18 is a special tribute to Alberto Giacometti, the sculptor and to Mark Rothko, the New York Abstract Expressionist whose huge maroon canvasses dominate the room. When wall space is at such a premium I find this allocation a little excessive but that is only a personal opinion. 18 apart, you can expect to see a chronological selection which may include works by any of the following painters, all of them somewhere in the collection if not actually on show on the day of your visit. Even in alphabetical order without comment, it is an impressive list: Albers, Appel, Auerbach, Bacon, Balla, Blake (Peter), Boccioni, Bomberg, Bonnard, Braque, Bratby, Buffet, Burra, Carra, Cezanne, Chagall, Chirico, Colquhoun, Crippa, Dali, Davie, Degas, De Kooning, Delaunay, Delvaux, Derain, De Stael, Dubuffet, Duchamp, Dufy, Ensor, Ernst, Fantin-Latour, Forain, Francis, Freud, Frost, Gauguin, Gottlieb, Gris, Heron, Hitchens, Hockney, Johns, Jones, Kandinsky, Kitaj, Klee, Kline, Kokoschka, Lanyon, Le Corbusier, Lewis, Lichtenstein, Leger, Louis, Lowry, Macbryde, Magritte, Manet, Marini, Masson, Matisse, Middleditch, Minton, Miro, Modigliani, Mondrian, Monet, Motherwell, Moynihan, Munch, Nash, Newman, Nicholson, Nolan, Noland, Nolde, Oldenburg, Pasmore, Permeke, Phillips (Peter), Phillips (Tom), Picasso, Piper, Pissarro, Poliakoff, Pollock, Rauschenberg, Ray, Redon, Renoir, Richards, Riley, Rivera, Roberts, Rothenstein, Rothko, Rouault, Rousseau, Schwitters, Severini, Seurat, Sisley, Smith, Soulages, Still, Sutherland, Tanguy, Tapies, Tobey, Toulouse-Lautrec, Utrillo, Van Gogh, Vasarely, Vaughan, Vuillard.

3
GOING WEST FROM PICCADILLY

The Royal Academy ✓

Burlington House, Piccadilly, W.1. (See map p. 126)
Telephone 01–734–9052
Opening Hours **Open only for the summer exhibition from May to July and special loan exhibitions at other times.** Hours during these periods: Monday to Saturday 10.00 to 18.00 and Sunday 14.00 to 18.00.
Closed **At all other times** and also Good Friday and Christmas Day.
Admission Charges vary according to the special exhibition but reductions for children, students and senior citizens. Season tickets issued.
Parking Very difficult.
How to get there **Underground:** Piccadilly Circus, Green Park. **Buses:** 9, 9a, 14, 19, 22, 25, 38, 506.
Facilities An excellent self-service restaurant in basement open only during exhibitions. Postcard counter.

Although the Royal Academy has a permanent collection, mostly of works submitted by distinguished academicians of the past such as Reynolds, Constable, Wilson and Gainsborough and also a few foreign works including Michangelo's tondo relief, it is shown only to research students who have made prior application, although new arrangements for public viewing may prevail in the future. The Academy is included here less for its tedious summer show than for its function as the home of some of London's most impressive temporary loan exhibitions. The visitor should check with the daily press to see if such an exhibition is being staged – if so, it will undoubtedly repay a visit. When the visit is made, take note of the entrance hall ceiling paintings by Angelica Kauffmann and Benjamin West, and the staircase decorations by Sebastiano Ricci.

The Museum of Mankind

The Ethnography Department of the British Museum,
6 Burlington Gardens, W.1. (See map p. 126)
Telephone 01–437–2224
Opening Hours Monday to Saturday 10.00 to 17.00, Sunday

14.30 to 18.00.
Closed Good Friday, Christmas Eve, Christmas Day, Boxing Day and New Year's Day.
Admission Free.
Parking Difficult.
How to get there From Piccadilly, tubes and buses as for the Royal Academy, then walk through the Burlington Arcade and turn right. From Regent Street, buses 3, 6, 12, 13, 39, 53, 59, 88, 159, 505, and then walk along Vigo Street.

Although the museum holds very little that could be called paintings, it has been included here because of the enormous influence primitive sculpture and objects have had on artists of our own time – Braque and Picasso, for example. If you wish to pursue such images, the museum shows Eskimo art, the aboriginal Gonds of central India, the Maya, African tribes including the Dogon and the Yoruba, and the Solomon Islanders among other changing displays.

Apsley House, The Wellington Museum

149 Piccadilly, Hyde Park Corner, W.1. (See map p. 126)
Telephone 01–499–5676
Opening Hours Monday to Saturday 10.00 to 18.00, Sunday 14.30 to 18.00
Closed Good Friday, Christmas Eve, Christmas Day, Boxing Day and New Year's Day.
Admission Free.
Parking A commercial car park in Park Lane, otherwise impossible.
How to get there **Underground**: Hyde Park Corner. **Buses**: 2, 2b, 9, 9a, 14, 16, 19, 22, 25, 26, 30, 36a, 36b, 38, 52, 73, 74, 74b, 137, 500.
Facilities No restaurant or coffee bar. Small postcard counter.

Apsley House was built by Robert Adam in the 1770's and was purchased by Arthur Wellesley, the famous Duke of Wellington from his own brother in 1817. Packed as it is with the spoils of war, and the tributes heaped on a long-serving politician who rose to be Prime Minister, it is now open to all-comers absolutely free,

APSLEY HOUSE

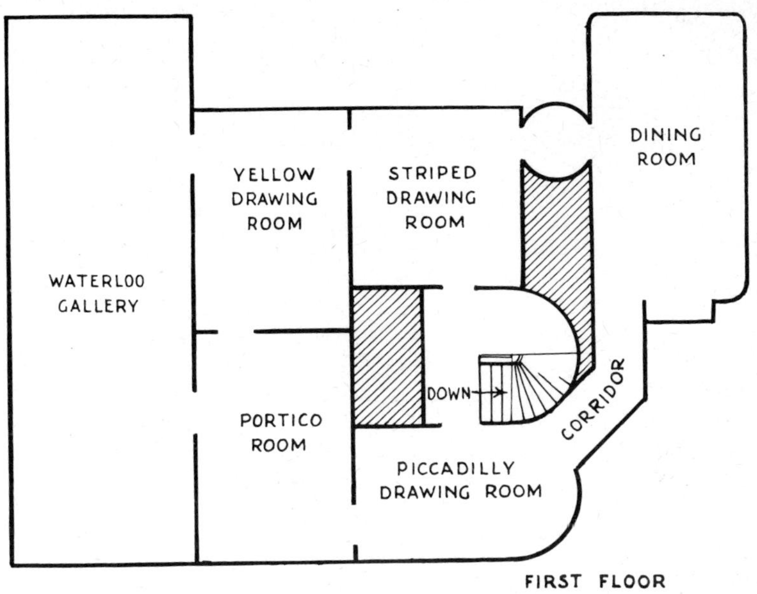

FIRST FLOOR

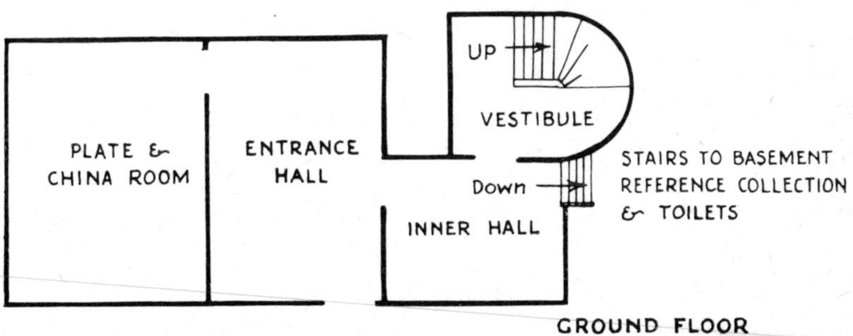

GROUND FLOOR

a democratic nicety of which the Iron Duke would undoubtedly have disapproved. The splendour of its collection is eloquent testimony to life as it was once lived by the rich and powerful. (In the Reform Bill agitation of 1832, the house was stoned by the mob as a symptom of wealth and privilege).

The entrance hall has Turner's *Tapping a Furnace* on the left hand wall (the casting taking place is of an equestrian statue of the Duke) and Landseer's large *Dialogue at Waterloo* on the right (with, of course, three obligatory Landseer dogs). Take a quick look at the plate and china room to the left of the hall if you are interested in porcelain, otherwise go into the Inner Hall on the right. The Inner Hall has some undistinguished portraits, and a lower staircase leading down to the basement which has a fine selection of caricatures of Wellington in every conceivable form from a boot to a lobster, and also ladies' and gentlemen's toilets. The stairs are hung with Sassoferrato's *Holy Family,* David Teniers the Younger's *View of a Chateau* (good) and Landseer's *The Illicit Still* (very bad). Come back up the stairs and turn right into the Staircase Vestibule, dominated by Canova's colossal marble statue of Wellington. Go up the main Wyatt staircase, hung with a number of Robert Lefevre portraits of the Bonapartes and pause on the first landing for Sir David Wilkie's large *William IV* portrait, and for his *Chelsea Pensioners reading the Waterloo Despatch*. To the left off the stairs is the green and gold Piccadilly Room full of interesting pictures. Look at Aert van der Neer's *River View: evening*, and Paul Brill's *Landscape with St Hubert and the Stag*, and then, to the left of the small fireplace, Marcellus Coffermans (?) *The Annunciation* and Adam Elsheimer's *Judith and Holofernes*. To the right of the fireplace are three by Jan Brueghel the Elder, *Entering the Ark, Road Scene with Figures* and *Travellers in a Landscape*. Between the windows see Vernet's *Shipwreck*, Abraham Storck's *Dutch shipping in a river*, and Van de Velde the Younger's *Large Ships and Boats in a Calm*. Also in the room are Cornelis van Poelenburgh's *Angels guiding the Shepherds*, the weird and disturbing *La Carcasse: a Witch being drawn to the Sabbath on the Skeleton of a Monster* (a work by José Ribera based on an engraving after Raphael and one to make some of Dali's post-Freudian fantasies thoroughly innocuous), Pieter de Hoogh's *A Cavalier talking to a Lady*, and Nicholas Maes' *Lovers with a Woman Listening*. On an easel in the middle of the room is Correggio's *Agony in the Garden*, a moving work with the light in the composition heavily concentrated in the top left hand corner.

Turn right into the green-damasked Portico Room (on the same side as the windows). It has a number of David Teniers the

Younger including *Landscape with Shepherds and Cattle, A Lime-Kiln with Figures* and *Interior of a Cow-House*. A pair of pictures by Luca Giordano, *Hagar in the Desert* and *Samson and Delilah*, are up above the doorways, and a pair by Jan Steen, *Wedding Party* and *Egg Dance*, are to left and right of the fireplace.

Take the exit opposite the fireplace and you will find yourself in the huge red Waterloo Gallery with banqueting table set with the dominating silver and silver-gilt Portugese service (itself 26 feet long) supplemented by two grey porphyry candelabra at either end of the table. If you had been a dinner guest in this most lavish of settings, your digestion might have been aided by the collection of paintings (many captured at the Battle of Vitoria). They include Murillo's *Portrait of an Unknown Man*, Claudio Coello's *St Catherine*, and to the left of the fireplace, Ribera's *St John the Baptist*. The vast *Charles I* above the fireplace is a copy of the Windsor Castle Van Dyck. To the right of the fireplace is a geniune Van Dyck in *St Rosalia*, and a Ribera *Santiago*. (i.e. St James himself not the South American city). The wall with the windows has a rich mixture of nationalities and periods with Trevisani's *Holy Family,* Claude's *Ponte Molle, near Rome* (too high on the wall to be seen properly), Salvator Rosa's *Battle Scene*, Rubens' *Head of an Old Man*, Reynolds' *Flight into Egypt*, Guido Reni's *St Joseph*, Murillo's *St Francis of Assisi*, two by Guiseppe Cesare (*Marriage of St Catherine* and *Expulsion from Paradise*), and Sassoferrato's *Virgin and Child*.

At the head of the room is the large and dramatic portrait of the great man himself – *Duke of Wellington on Horseback* by Goya. Retire from the Waterloo Gallery into the Yellow Drawing Room which has a smaller and more select group of canvasses. To the left of the fireplace is *Ana Dorothea, daughter of Rudolph II as a nun* by Rubens, and above the fireplace is perhaps the finest work in the house – *The Water Seller of Seville* by Velazquez. Look if you will at the brush-strokes on the face and sleeve of the water-seller, at the stain on the pitcher and at the general lighting scheme to see the influence of Caravaggio's style of realism upon Velazquez, and for what he himself added to it. Two other works by Velazquez are nearby on the right, *Spanish Gentleman* and *Pope Innocent X* (ascribed). Also here are Murillo's *Isaac Blessing Jacob,* Philip Wouverman's *Departure of a Hawking Party* and another fine Velazquez, *Two Young Men Eating at a Humble Table*, where the utensils take precedence over the young men.

The next room, the Striped Drawing Room is less fortunate in artistic standards but see Lawrence's version of *The Duke of Wellington* over the fireplace, and his portraits of *Henry William Paget,* of *Thomas Graham,* and of *William Carr.* Take the door to the left of the fireplace into the Dining-Room for David Wilkie's *George IV*, in full Scottish regalia more suitable for painter than subject, and poorly drawn. Outside the room, the corridor leads back to the Piccadilly Drawing Room. It has an unknown Flemish artist's *Self-Portrait* and some more Dutch seventeenth century landscapes.

In a Hurry Apsley House is quite a small collection if seen in its entirety, but if you are only able to spend a very short time, try to see the following: the Turner *Tapping a Furnace* (Entrance hall); the main staircase with Canova's statue; and on the first floor, Correggio's *Agony in the Garden* on the easel in the Piccadilly Drawing Room; in the Waterloo Gallery Goya's very large *Duke of Wellington* – the room itself should be seen anyway – and, in the Yellow Drawing Room, both Velazquez's *Water Seller of Seville* and his *Two Young Men eating at a Humble Table*.

The Queen's Gallery ✓

Buckingham Palace, Buckingham Palace Road, S.W.1.
Opening Hours **Only during special exhibitions** – Tuesday to Saturday 11.00 to 17.00 (the same hours apply for Easter Sunday, Easter Monday, Spring Bank Holiday and Late Summer Bank Holiday). Sunday 14.00 to 17.00
Closed **At all times when there is no exhibition and always on Mondays.**
Admission Charges vary according to the special exhibition.
Parking Don't
How to get there **Underground:** Victoria and walk along Buckingham Palace Road towards Buckingham Palace – the Gallery entrance is on the left. **Buses:** 2, 2b, 10a, 11, 16, 24, 25, 26, 29, 36, 36a, 36b, 38, 39, 52, 149, 181, 185, 500, 503, 506, 507.
Facilities Small postcard and souvenir book counter.

The Queen's Gallery, entered from Buckingham Palace Road, was formed by the conversion of the westerly part of the private chapel in the southern wing of Buckingham Palace. Its function is to stage special exhibitions of paintings, drawings and *objets d'art* drawn from the monarch's fabulous private collections which are normally scattered throughout Hampton Court, Windsor Castle, Kensington Palace, Buckingham Palace and the other Royal residences, some items regularly in public view and others very rarely seen. Closed except when there is an exhibition in progress, the gallery takes a theme – 'George III as Collector and Patron', for example, the 1974–5 exhibition – and illustrates it from the collections. Always worth a visit when a show is in progress.

The London Museum/A Special Note

Regular visitors to London, and even some residents, may wonder at the omission of the London Museum from this guide. The reason is neither an oversight nor a slight to its excellent collection, but because the museum itself will be without a home for some time. The collection formerly held by the Guildhall Museum of the City of London, and the one held by the London Museum at Kensington Palace, are to be combined to form a new Museum of London. This new museum is to open on a special site at the junction of Aldersgate St and London Wall at the Barbican in late 1975 or early 1976. In the meantime contact the Museum of London, Condor House 13–14 St Paul's Churchyard, London E.C.4 (Telephone 01–236–2145) with any enquiries.

Leighton House

12 Holland Park Road, W.14. (See map p.48)
Telephone 01–602–3316.
Opening Hours Monday to Saturday 11.00 to 17.00
Closed SUNDAYS, and Good Friday, Easter Saturday, Easter Monday, Spring Bank Holiday, Late Summer Bank Holiday, Christmas Day, Boxing Day, and New Year's Day.
Admission Free.
Parking Area subject to residents' only parking, but you may be lucky and find a gap nearby.
How to get there **Underground**: High Street Kensington (Holland

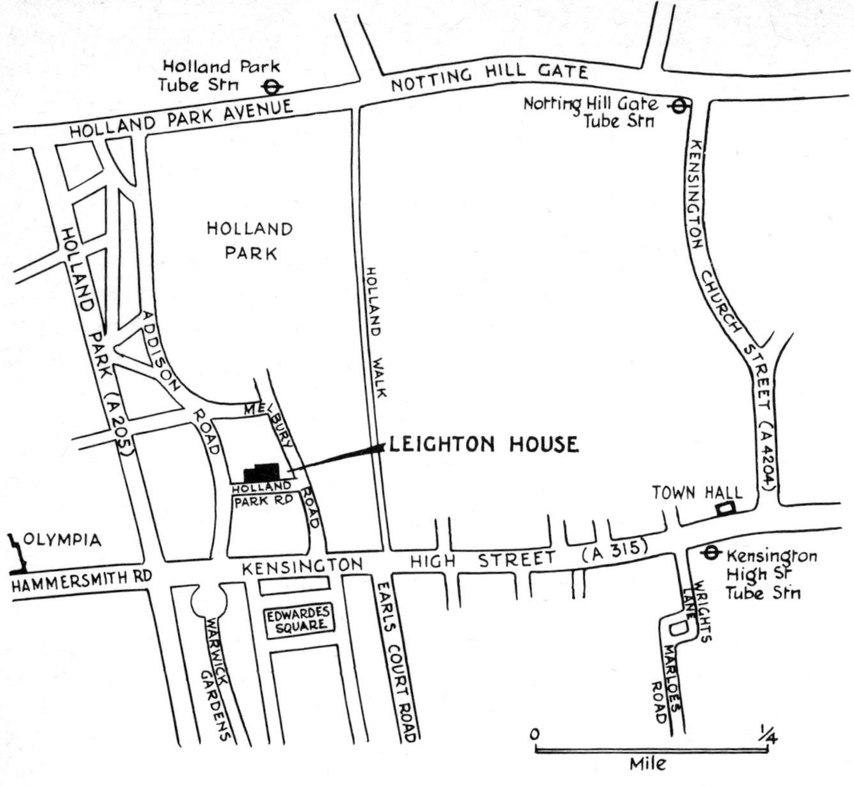

Park station about a mile away). **Buses**: 9, 9a, 27, 28, 33, 49, 73.

The architect of 12 Holland Park Road was George Aitchinson, but the house is really the painterly needs and imaginative fantasies of a wealthy Victorian bachelor translated into reality. Lord Leighton (1830–1896), painter, sculptor, President of the Royal Academy and the only painter ever to be elevated to the peerage (hard luck, Constable, Turner, Reynolds and Co.), had this house built in 1866 as a combined studio and residence. Apart from its intrinsic interest as incorporating a piece of exotic Victorian interior design, it has a fine selection of Victorian paintings by Leighton and his contemporaries.

The entrance hall shows a School of Tintoretto *Apotheosis of Marc Antonio Bragadin* and a Leighton *Portrait of his father.*

Now visit the Arab Hall to the left coming out of the entrance hall. It has no paintings but look at its decorative oriental tiles imported from Northern Africa by Leighton and Sir Richard Burton (who perhaps concealed them under the pornography in his suitcase) and providing an exotic background to the sound of the tinkling jet fountain which feeds the black marble pool in the floor, the whole like some strange mosque transported to W.14. Also on the ground floor the drawing room contains a Burne-Jones version of *King Cophetua and the Beggar Maid* quite unlike that in the Tate, a S.J. Solomon *Conversation Piece*, Val Prinsep's *Ayesha*, and two Leightons – *Young Lord Wellesley* and *Noble Lady of Venice*. The dining room houses Mrs Russell Barrington's Rossetti-like *Seated Lady*, and H. Herkomer's *Found* (difficult to see through the glass).

Ascend the stairs with its stuffed peacock and more Leightons, including a strange copy of Michelangelo's figures from the Sistine Chapel ceiling, and go into the bedroom to the left for more Leighton studies. The open-plan area next to the bedroom is the 'Music Room' and has Ford Madox Brown's *Study for the Execution of Mary, Queen of Scots*, Leighton's *Elisha raising the son of the Shunammite* (over the fireplace), *Bianca* and *Pavana*, Watts' *Brynhylda* and *Portrait of Dorothy Tennant*, Alma-Tadema's *Sunday Morning*, Alfred Stevens' *W.B. Spence*, Alma-Tadema's excuse for some nude ladies, *A Favourite Custom*, and Poynter's excuse for a nude boy, *Outward Bound*.

The Painting Room, the continuation of the Music Room, displays Ford Madox Brown's *Head* (a superb profile this), a J.F. Lewis *The Harem* (not far removed from the Arab Hall downstairs) and two water-colour gouaches by Burne-Jones, *Sir Launcelot* and *Sir Percival and Sir Bors*.

The remaining room on the first floor is the very large studio (now often used for local society functions and the like). It holds Whistler's *Miss Alexander*, Leighton's *Bath of Psyche*, Millais' sentimental *Portrait of Robert Rankin* (all long ginger hair and green velvet suit), Leighton's *Clytemnestra*, Millais' card playing ladies *Hearts are Trumps*, Poynter's *Visit to Aesculapius* with four naked ladies, perhaps the three graces and a first reserve, Watts' tortured male nude *Chaos*, Leighton's formidable lady *Coruna of Tangra*, and, perhaps deserving of a blue riband for sentimentality, banality and suppressed sexuality, Anna Lea Merritt's *Love*

Locked Out which it takes the Burne-Jones *Morning of the Resurrection* with a solemn Jesus in profile to erase from the memory.

4
SOUTH KENSINGTON

The Victoria and Albert Museum

Cromwell Road, South Kensington, S.W.7. (See map p.54)
Telephone 01-589-6371
Opening Hours Monday to Saturday 10.00 to 18.00. Sunday 14.30 to 18.00 (including Easter Sunday).
Closed Good Friday, Christmas Eve, Christmas Day, Boxing Day, New Year's Day.
Admission Free.
Parking Some meters in the vicinity.
How to get there **Underground**: South Kensington (there is an underground tunnel direct from the station to the museum but the entrance is not always open). **Buses**: 14, 30, 39a, 45, 49, 74, 74b.
Facilities Information counter in entrance hall from Exhibition Road. Books and postcard counter. Craft shop. Restaurant (waitress service) and self-service cafeteria open 10.00 to 14.30 and 15.00 to 17.30 weekdays; and 14.30 to 17.30 on Sundays. Free lectures on Saturday at 15.00 and on Monday, Wednesday and Friday at 13.15 – check with the museum for details. The V & A also has one of the finest art libraries in the world.

To put it simply, the Victoria and Albert Museum is a vast treasurehouse of applied art, no less than 145 rooms stuffed to the seams with art of all kinds, all periods and all countries. If its rooms were put end to end they would stretch for about six miles, so one can perhaps be forgiven for having to condense its glories rigorously lest they threaten to swamp this little book completely. If you do not have at least two days to devote to its study, I suggest you study the accompanying floor plans (pp. 58 & 59) and visit those galleries which particularly appeal but resign yourself to getting lost from time to time. What follows is a little guided tour for those primarily interested in painting to the major rooms of interest and to a few odd corners which might otherwise escape notice.

From the main entrance in Cromwell Road, go left to the bookstall and left again through the architectural collection to 48 and the seven Raphael Cartoons. One of the greatest glories of the Royal Collection and loaned to the V & A since 1865, each of these vast gouache cartoons is composed of anything up to 200 overlapping pieces of paper pasted on a canvas backing. Their

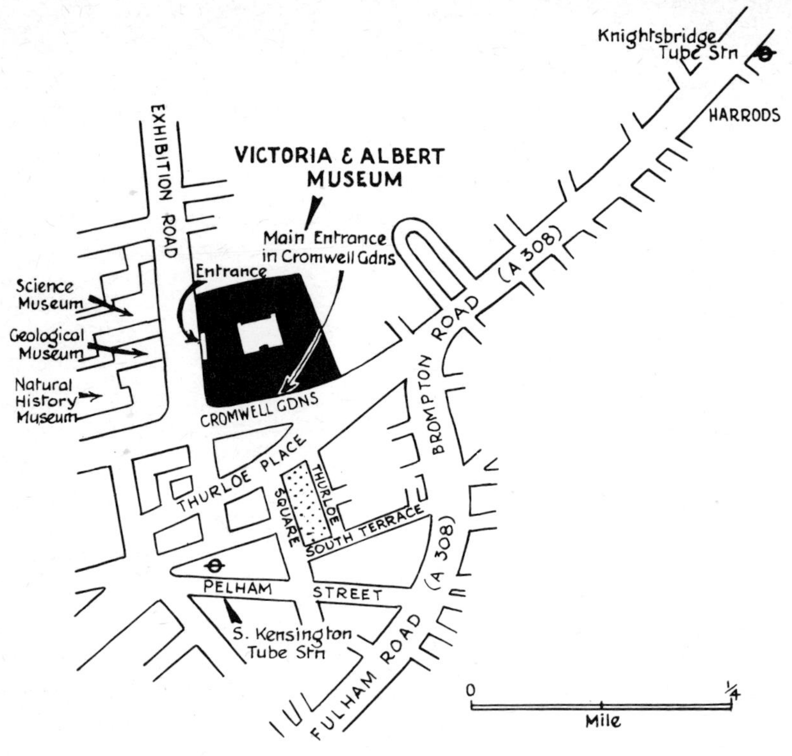

purpose was to provide a working base for the weaving of the tapestries now exhibited in the Vatican Pinacoteca and originally intended for the Sistine Chapel which meant competing with Michelangelo's frescoes, a task only a Raphael could face with relative equanimity. If you wish to prepare yourself adequately for this part of Raphael's contribution to the High Renaissance, you may like to know that the subjects and their biblical starting points are as follows – *The Miraculous Draught of Fishes* (Luke V 3–10); *Christ's Charge to Peter* (John XXI 15–17); *Healing of the Lame Man* (Acts III 1–11); *Death of Ananias* (Acts V 1–6); *The Blinding of Elymas the Magician* (Acts XIII 1–11); *The Sacrifice at Lystra* (Acts XIV 8–18); and *St Paul Preaching at Athens* (Acts XVII 15–34). (Three others all based on incidents in Acts have been lost).

When looking at the cartoons themselves, two adjustments have to be made by the spectator – although the strength of the light in the gallery is electronically controlled, some of the pigments (actually Raphael used only ten pigments throughout) have faded so we are seeing a less colourful display than we would otherwise. (This explains the oddity in the *Miraculous Draught* where Christ's robe is white, yet its reflection in the water is a pinky-red). Also, the nature of the process of tapestry weaving meant that these designs are *in reverse* to the tapestries themselves. In the *Miraculous Draught*, for example, Christ is meant to appear on the *left* of the final tapestry, and raises his *right* hand to Simon Peter.

From the cartoon gallery take the stairs up to 57 and 57a and contrast the tremendous scale of the Raphaels with the tiny English miniatures of about 1700 to 1850, and do not miss the earlier ones of 1540–1750 which can be seen by walking through 56 to the darkened 55. Here are Holbein's *Mrs Pemberton* and *Anne of Cleves*, Nicholas Hilliard's *Self-portrait* and *Young Man leaning against a tree*, Isaac Oliver's *Countess of Somerset*, Samuel Cooper's *James II* and *Anthony Ashley* and Nicholas Dixon's *Charles Churchill*. Retrace your steps to 57 and go back down the steps to the Raphaels. Take the exit opposite into 47a, turn right and then first left into 41 for Indian art. Here the bays include some staggeringly beautiful Mughal paintings – a wholly different set of pictorial conventions from Western art and leading, see Bay 6, to some nineteenth century works that look very modern indeed. Exit from the opposite end of 41 into the long Renaissance and Gothic corridor. Cross it into 20 and Renaissance Italy and follow the rooms through 20, 19, 18, 17 (which has a Carlo Crivelli *Virgin and Child*), 11 (which has an Antonello Da Saliba *Crucifix*), 12, 13 (which has the William Morris room off to the left), 15, 16, 27 (which has a German painted and carved altarpiece *Legend of St Margaret*) and 26. Now turn left through the glass panelled door into 38 and the Gothic tapestries. Not only does this room have some spectacular tapestries, it has a spectacular Flemish carved altarpiece from the early sixteenth century, and on the back of one of the free standing partitions is the *Triptych with the Annunciation* by the *Flemish* Master of the St Ursula Legend. Take the other exit from 38 and you are in 38a which may have a temporary exhibition but, more importantly, is opposite the cafeteria and resturant for a coffee break. That over, come out and turn left into the carpets corridor. Turn right and walk along until you come to the stairs on your left (25). A few yards further on in 24, to the left is a glass case which contains a rare German tempera panel *Altarpiece of the Apocalypse*, from the workshop of Meister Bertram. It is a kind of Gothic strip cartoon illustrating the Book of Revelations and deriving its interpretations from a medieval Commentary on the Apocalypse. The pictures are to be read from left to right across the whole width of the work and are full of iconographical details for deciphering – for example, in the fourth picture from the left, the rainbow represents Christ's power over Earth and Heaven, the 24 figures represent the heads of churches, the seven lamps are the Holy Ghost, and the four animals perhaps the four evangelists.

Retrace your steps to 25 and the stairs. Do not climb the stairs until you have studied the very large Spanish altarpiece which features scenes from the life of *St George*, its gory and sadistic detail belied by the richness of the gold and the colourful paint. (It has been undergoing piecemeal cleaning and restoration for some time). Go up the stairs and turn right through 84, 83, 89, 82, and 81, then turn right into 87 which features foreign paintings (It is impossible to show all of the large collection of paintings held by the V & A at any one time, so that the painting rooms are particularly *subject to change without notice*. Should you wish to see a specific work not on show, apply to the print room and paintings office off Room 71). Normally, 87 will show Canaletto's *Capriccio*, Jan Brueghel the Elder's excellent *The Garden of Eden*, Pedro Romana's *Annunciation,* Beccafumi's *Conversion of St Paul* and, for me one of the most interesting pictures in the collection, by the Master of the St Ursula Legend (*of Cologne*) *The Martyrdom of St Ursula and the 11,000 Virgins*. Bought in the 1850's for 30 gns as a useful reference to costume, only later was it realised that the work was a part of a cycle of perhaps 20 or so canvasses on the St Ursula legend, others have emerged in various places on the continent. (Of dubious veracity, the Ursula legend tells of Ursula the virgin sailing to Rome with 11,000 virgins to avoid an unwanted suitor, and landing at Cologne on her return at the time that the Huns were putting the city under siege. She and her companions were martyred rather than see her 'married', this time to the King of the Huns). In this picture, the central dying figure is Etherius, the original unwanted suitor, the background is Cologne, and the dreaded Hun figures prominently.

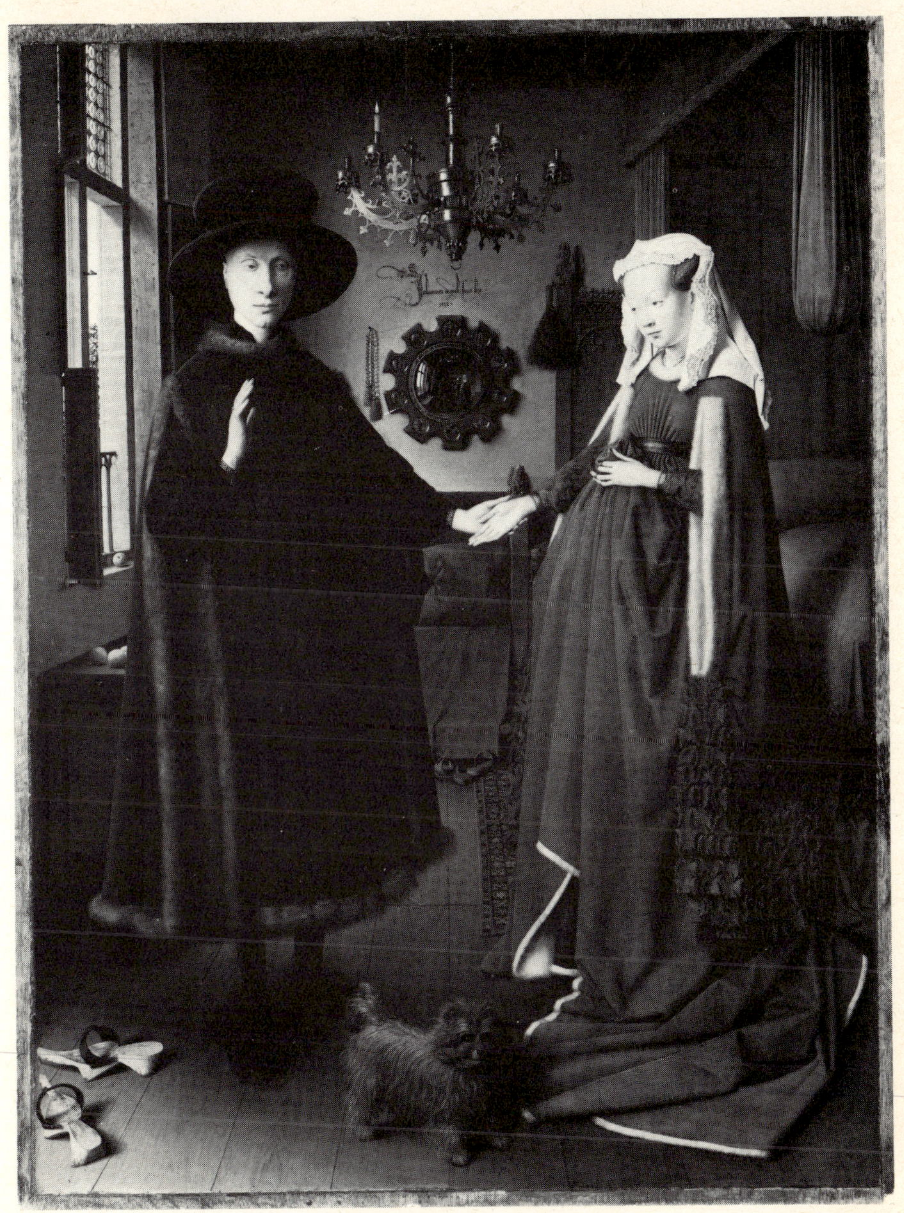

The Arnolfini Marriage by Jan Van Eyck, *The National Gallery*

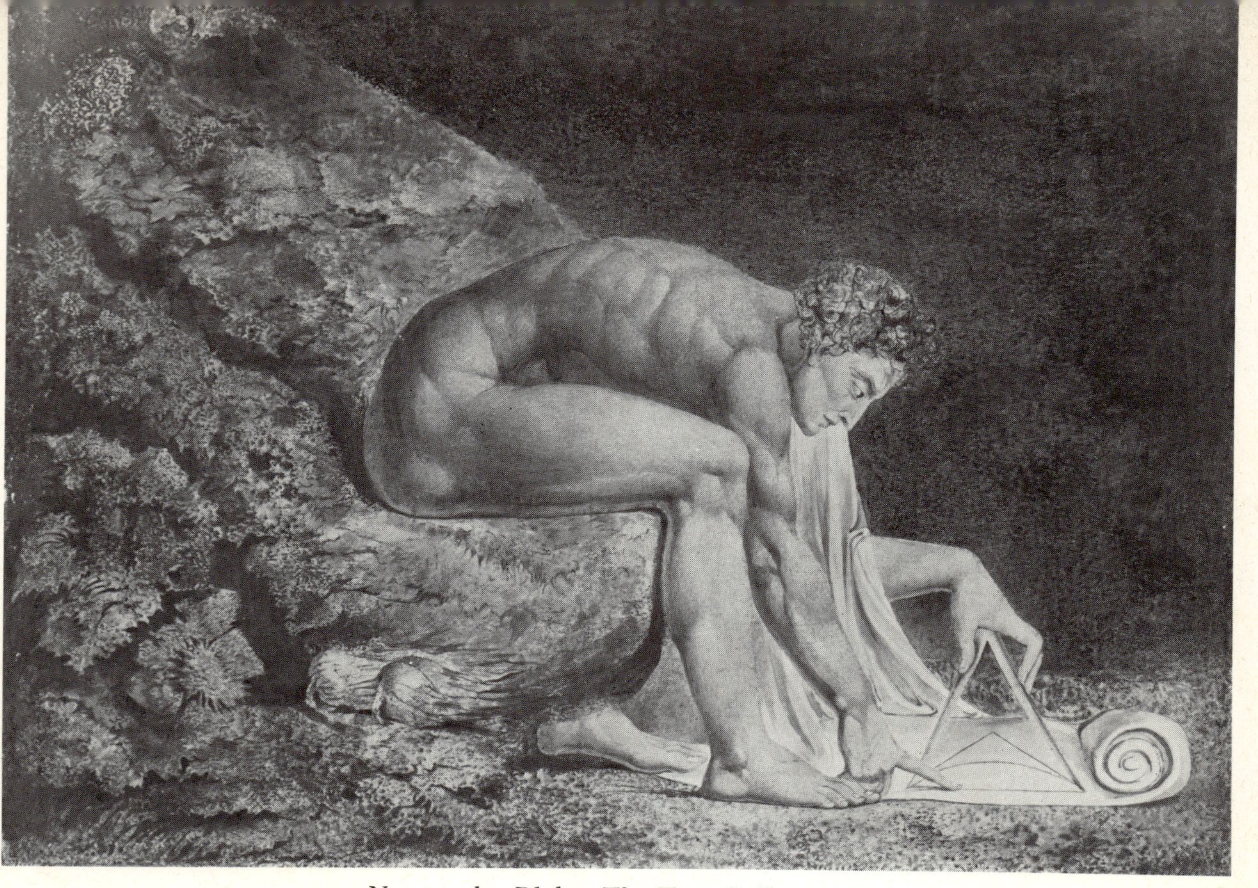

Newton by Blake, *The Tate Gallery*

Push open the glass doors and enter the long tapestry gallery. Halfway along on the right is the entrance to 105 and to the group of painting rooms. Room 105 has the Ionides collection (donated in 1901 by the man whose family features in the G.F. Watts' portraits in the room). This has Nardo Di Cione's *Coronation of the Virgin*, Rembrandt's *Departure of the Shunammite Woman*, Poussin's *Artists Sketching amongst Ruins*, Fantin-Latour's *Flowers*, Degas' first class theatre scene *Ballet from Roberto il Diavolo,* Delacroix's *Good Samaritan,* Courbet's *L'Immensité,* Millet's *The Wood Sawyers*, Louis le Nain's *Landscape with Figures*, Alma-Tadema's *The Visit*, D.G. Rossetti's *The Day Dream* (one of the best Rossettis in London), and Burne-Jones' *The Mill*.

The adjoining 104b (green) has a striking Fuseli *The Fire King*, some Richard Wilsons, some George Morlands, Gainsborough's *Daughters*, and a Thornhill sketch for his work at Greenwich (see p. 102). 104a (red) and 104 move from eighteenth century to the nineteenth with two Landseers, *Suspense* (with dog) and *The Old Shepherd's Chief Mourner* (yes, another dog), James Ward's *Bull Fighting* (with the bulls sublimated to the romantic landscape – remember Ward's *Gordale Scar* in the Tate and compare the two), a large group of William Mulready's genre paintings, another of C.R. Leslie's (though Leslie is better known now as Constable's first biographer than as a painter in his own right), Turner's *Venice* and *Lifeboat*, P. de Wint's *Woody Landscape* and Etty's *The Deluge* (the inevitable Etty naked lady).

This brings us to 103 featuring one of the museum's most prized collections. Donated in 1888 by the painter's daughter, nearly 100 characteristic oil sketches by the great Constable are hung here (including a lively full-scale study for *The Leaping Horse*) painted with freshness and immediacy and making this room perhaps the world's centre for Constable studies. *Study for the Hay Wain, Boat-building near Flatford Mill, Hampstead Heath*, and *Salisbury Cathedral* are all included. 106a (pale green) features a representative selection of the 300 or so watercolours and drawings included in the Constable gift.

Water-colours are also shown in 106b with most of the early nineteenth century English artists represented who brought the art to a kind of perfection unrealised elsewhere – perhaps changeability of the English climate and the quickness of the medium are

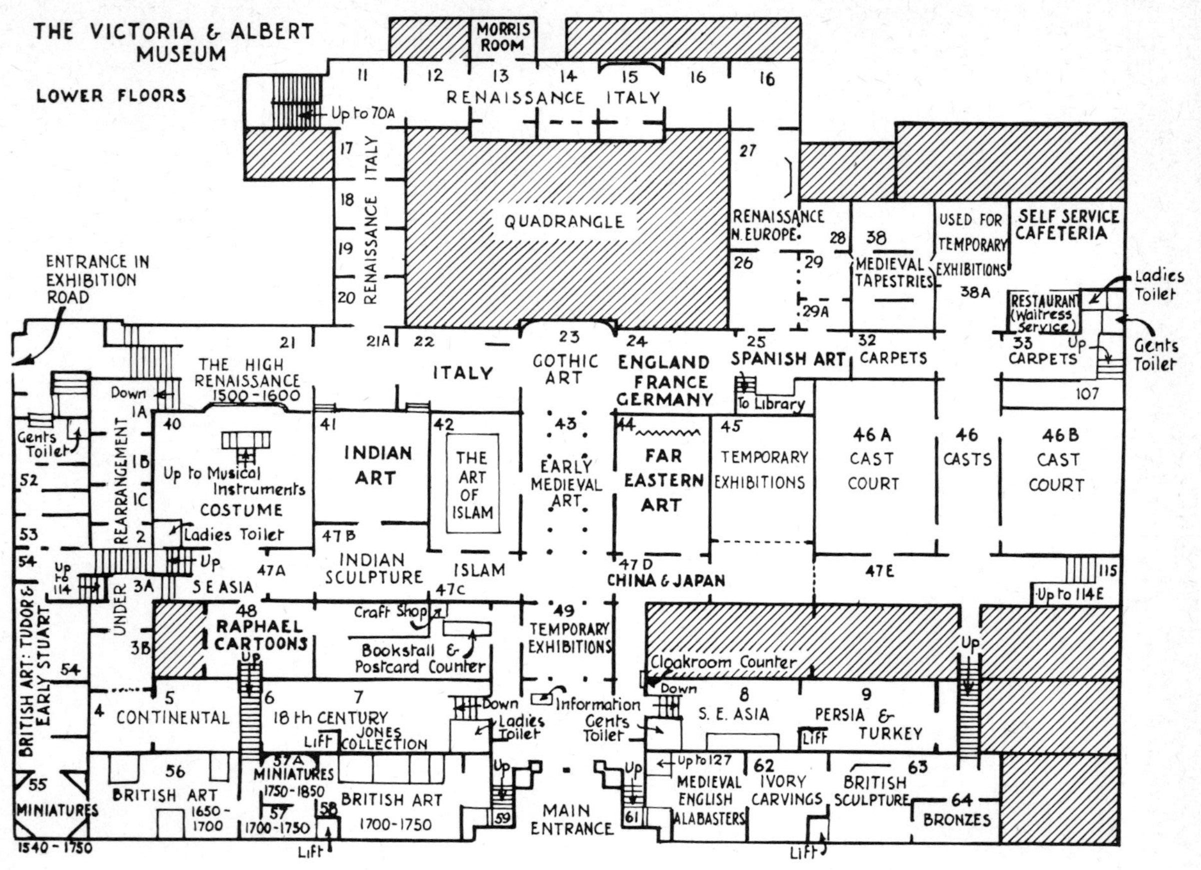

THE VICTORIA & ALBERT MUSEUM
LOWER FLOORS
MORRIS ROOM
RENAISSANCE ITALY
Up to 70A
RENAISSANCE ITALY
QUADRANGLE
ENTRANCE IN EXHIBITION ROAD
RENAISSANCE N. EUROPE
38 MEDIEVAL TAPESTRIES
USED FOR TEMPORARY EXHIBITIONS 38A
SELF SERVICE CAFETERIA
RESTAURANT (Waitress Service)
Ladies Toilet
Gents Toilet
THE HIGH RENAISSANCE 1500-1600
ITALY
GOTHIC ART
ENGLAND FRANCE GERMANY
SPANISH ART
CARPETS
33 CARPETS
To Library
107
Down
Gents Toilet
REARRANGEMENT
Up to Musical Instruments
COSTUME
Ladies Toilet
INDIAN ART
THE ART OF ISLAM
EARLY MEDIEVAL ART
FAR EASTERN ART
TEMPORARY EXHIBITIONS
46 A CAST COURT
46 CASTS
46 B CAST COURT
Up to 114
S E ASIA
INDIAN SCULPTURE
ISLAM
47 D CHINA & JAPAN
47E
Up to 114E
UNDER
48 RAPHAEL CARTOONS
Craft Shop
Bookstall & Postcard Counter
49 TEMPORARY EXHIBITIONS
Cloakroom Counter
BRITISH ART: TUDOR & EARLY STUART
CONTINENTAL
18 th CENTURY
JONES COLLECTION
Lift
Information
Ladies Toilet
Gents Toilet
8 S. E. ASIA
9 PERSIA & TURKEY
57A MINIATURES 1750-1850
56 BRITISH ART 1650-1700
57 1700-1750
58 BRITISH ART 1700-1750
55 MINIATURES 1540-1750
MAIN ENTRANCE
Up to 127
MEDIEVAL ENGLISH ALABASTERS
62 IVORY CARVINGS
63 BRITISH SCULPTURE
64 BRONZES

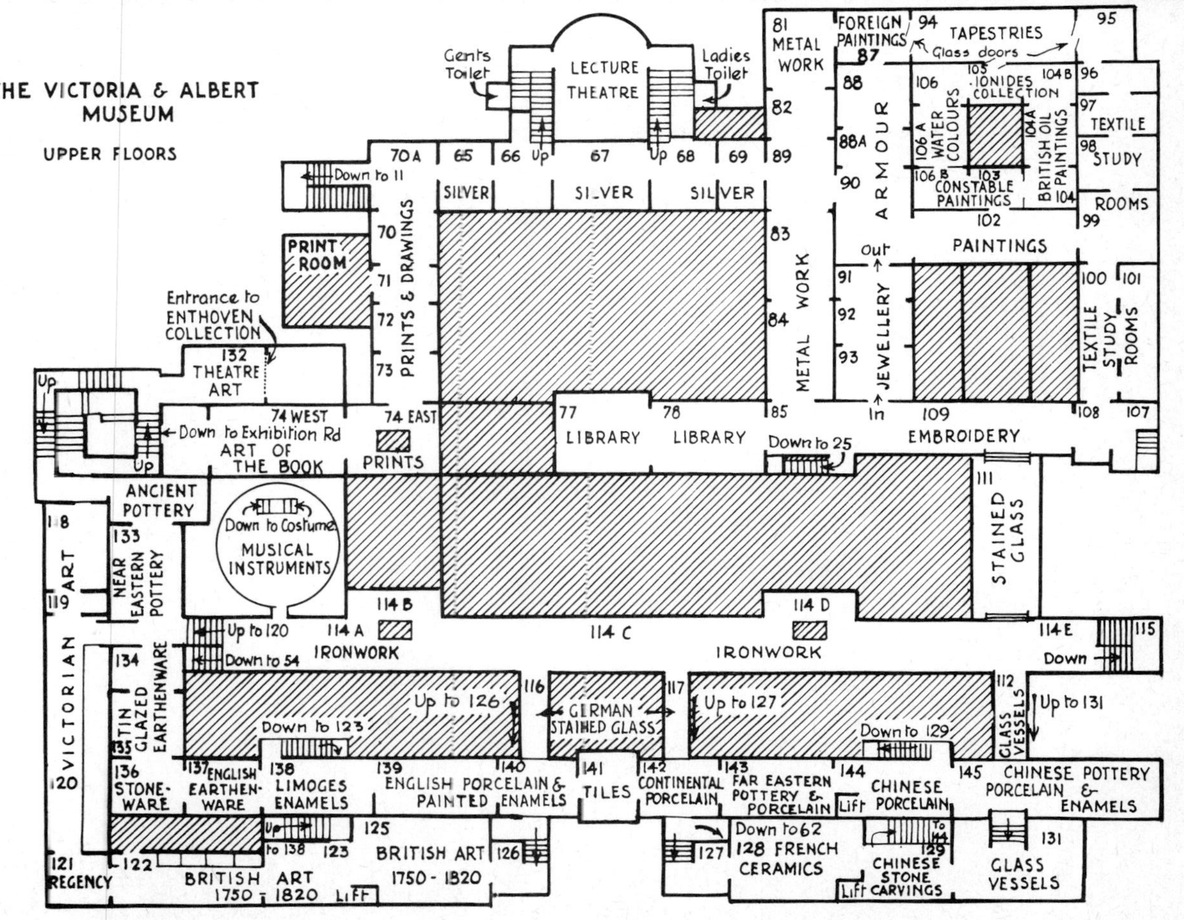
THE VICTORIA & ALBERT MUSEUM
UPPER FLOORS
Gents Toilet
LECTURE THEATRE
Ladies Toilet
70A
65
66
Up
67
Up
68
69
89
Down to 11
SILVER
SI_VER
SILVER
70
71
72
73
PRINTS & DRAWINGS
PRINT ROOM
Entrance to ENTHOVEN COLLECTION
132 THEATRE ART
74 WEST
74 EAST
Up
Down to Exhibition Rd
Up
ART OF THE BOOK
PRINTS
77
LIBRARY
78
LIBRARY
81 METAL WORK
82
83
84
85
METAL WORK
Down to 25
FOREIGN PAINTINGS 87
94
TAPESTRIES
Glass doors
95
88
88A
90
ARMOUR
106
105 IONIDES COLLECTION
104 B
106 A WATER COLOURS
104A
BRITISH OIL PAINTINGS
106 B
103 CONSTABLE PAINTINGS
104
102
96
97 TEXTILE
98 STUDY
ROOMS
99
PAINTINGS
Out
91
92
93
JEWELLERY
In
100
101
TEXTILE STUDY ROOMS
109
EMBROIDERY
108
107
111
STAINED GLASS
ANCIENT POTTERY
Down to Costume
MUSICAL INSTRUMENTS
118
133
NEAR EASTERN POTTERY
ART
119
VICTORIAN
114 B
114 A
114 C
114 D
IRONWORK
Up to 120
Down to 54
IRONWORK
114 E
115
Down
134
TIN GLAZED EARTHENWARE
135
Up to 126
116
GERMAN STAINED GLASS
117
Up to 127
112
GLASS VESSELS
Up to 131
Down to 123
Down to 129
120
136 STONE-WARE
137 ENGLISH EARTHEN-WARE
138 LIMOGES ENAMELS
139 ENGLISH PORCELAIN & PAINTED ENAMELS
140
141 TILES
142 CONTINENTAL PORCELAIN
143 FAR EASTERN POTTERY & PORCELAIN
144 CHINESE PORCELAIN
Lift
145 CHINESE POTTERY PORCELAIN & ENAMELS
Up
to 138
125
123
BRITISH ART
126
127
Down to 62
128 FRENCH CERAMICS
To 144
129
CHINESE STONE CARVINGS
Lift
131
GLASS VESSELS
121 REGENCY
122
BRITISH ART 1750 - 1820
LIFT
1750 - 1820

linked. Anyway here are Turner, John Linnell, Samuel Palmer, John Sell Cotman, John Robert Cozens, and the hallucinatory *Naomi entreating Ruth and Orpah to return to the land of Moab* which even the title alone would give away as being by William Blake. In 106, watercolours continue with some twentieth century names taking over, including Paul Nash, David Jones, Wyndham Lewis, Emil Nolde, Peter Blake, Bridget Riley and Fernand Leger.

If time permits, a pleasant way to see a sample of paintings in period settings is to leave the painting rooms by the exit in the Constable room, turn left past the Burne-Jones' panel *The Car of Love* and turn right through the textile study rooms to 108. At 108 turn right and then left through the stained glass tunnel. At the end turn right into the long ironwork corridor and walk along it to the *second* stained glass tunnel on the left (116). Walk through it and walk up the stairs at the end. Turn right into Room 126 and begin to follow the rooms through 125, 123, 122, 121, 120, 119, and 118. These are arranged in chonological order from the 1750's to the late Victorian era, and feature interiors, furniture, wall and floor decorations and the like, including paintings, some of them of high quality, and forming a useful reminder that the works were meant not for the museum but for the home. The stairs at the end lead down to the Exhibition Road exit.

5
WEST CENTRAL

The British Museum

Great Russell Street, W.C.1 (See map p.64).
Telephone 01–636–1555
Opening Hours Monday to Saturday 10.00 to 17.00, Sunday 14.30 to 18.00.
Closed Good Friday, Christmas Eve, Christmas Day, Boxing Day, and New Year's Day.
Admission Free.
Parking The Museum forecourt is partly allocated to parking but the space is heavily used and 'car park full' is a notice used very often. Commercial car parks in the vicinity.
How to get there **Underground**: Tottenham Court Road, Goodge Street, Russell Square, Holborn, Euston Square (From Euston Square, Russell Square and Goodge Street it is probably best to use the North Entrance to the Museum in Montague Place). **Buses**: 68, 77, 77a, 77c, 170, 188 (to Southampton Row, get off at Great Russell Street); 7, 8, 19, 22, 25, 38 (to New Oxford Street, get off at Museum Street); 14, 24, 29, 73, 176 to Gower Street (when going south) or to Tottenham Court Road (when going north) in both cases get off at Great Russell St; 172 to Southampton Place.
Facilities The tea and coffee room in the basement offers machine-dispensed beverages only. Counters on the ground floor offer postcards, booklets and souvenir replicas. Free lectures are held regularly in most of the museum's departments usually at 13.15 or 15.00 but obtain subjects and details from the Museum.

One of the greatest of national assets, the British Museum offers a unique blend of history, literature, archaeology and art. Behind its stately grey portico are invaluable quarries for the student and serious researcher like the Reading Room and North Library (which have about 8 million books) and the Students' rooms for the department of Manuscripts, Oriental Printed Books and Manuscripts, and Prints and Drawings (all of them open only to holders of special tickets); and also main display collections which display the cream skimmed from vast holdings under the headings of Greek and Roman Antiquities, Egyptian Antiquities, Prehistoric and Romano-British Antiquities, Western Asiatic Antiquities, Coins and Medals, Oriental Antiquities, and Medieval and Later Antiquities (the last category a misleading but all-embracing title

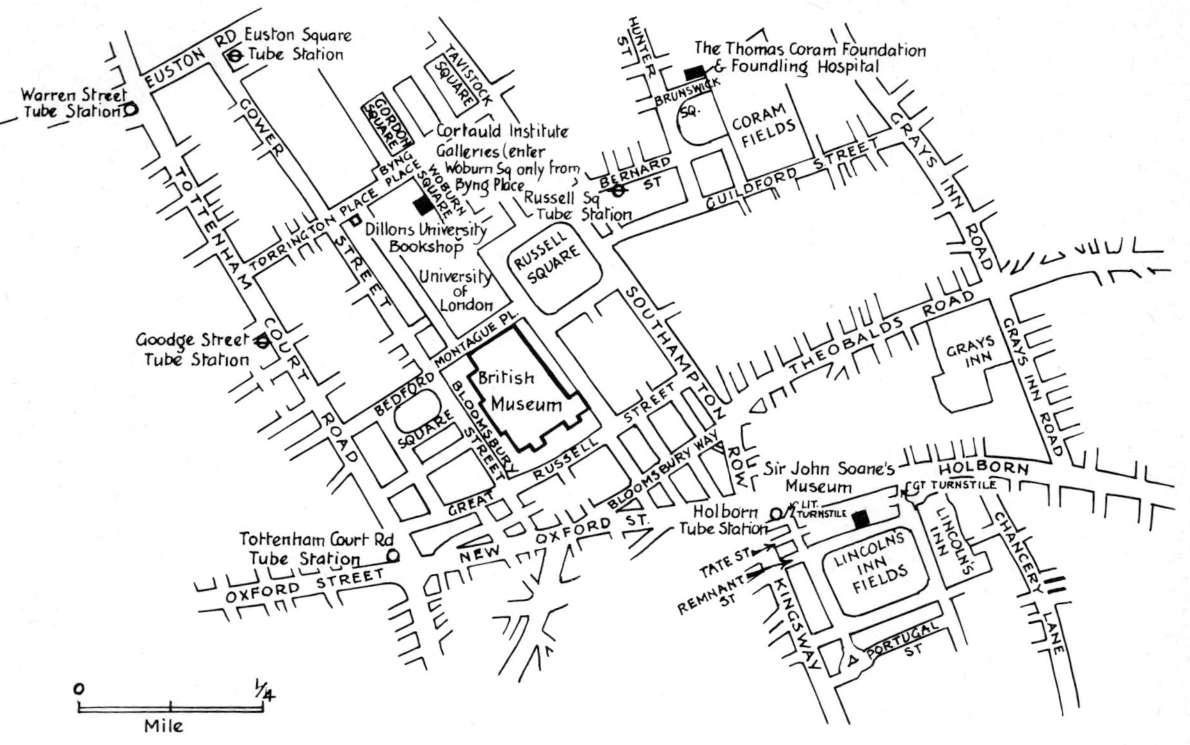

Warren Street
Tube Station
EUSTON RD
Euston Square
Tube Station
TAVISTOCK SQUARE
GORDON SQUARE
Cortauld Institute
Galleries (enter
Woburn Sq only from
Byng Place)
HUNTER ST
BRUNSWICK SQ.
The Thomas Coram Foundation
& Foundling Hospital
CORAM FIELDS
BERNARD ST
Russell Sq
Tube Station
GUILDFORD STREET
GRAYS INN ROAD
COWER
BYNG PLACE
WOBURN SQUARE
TORRINGTON PLACE
Dillons University
Bookshop
University
of
London
RUSSELL SQUARE
TOTTENHAM COURT ROAD
STREET
MONTAGUE PL.
SOUTHAMPTON ROW
THEOBALDS ROAD
GRAYS INN
GRAYS INN ROAD
Goodge Street
Tube Station
BEDFORD SQUARE
British
Museum
BLOOMSBURY STREET
STREET
GREAT RUSSELL
BLOOMSBURY WAY
Sir John Soane's
Museum
HOLBORN
GT TURNSTILE
LIT. TURNSTILE
Holborn
Tube Station
NEW OXFORD ST.
Tottenham Court Rd
Tube Station
OXFORD STREET
TATE ST
REMNANT ST
KINGSWAY
LINCOLNS INN FIELDS
LINCOLN'S INN
CHANCERY LANE
PORTUGAL ST
0
1/4
Mile

THE BRITISH MUSEUM
GROUND FLOOR

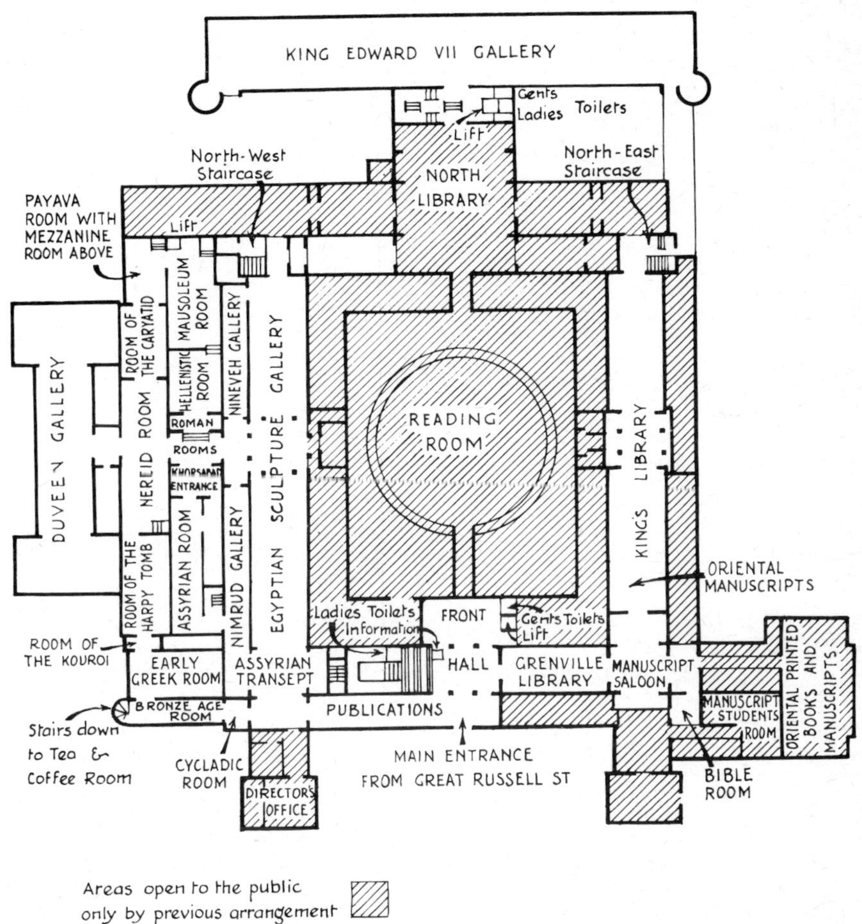

including jewellery, clocks and porcelain and the like). Like the V & A, miles of galleries offer the splendid possibility of getting lost amongst some of the world's greatest treasures, though admittedly

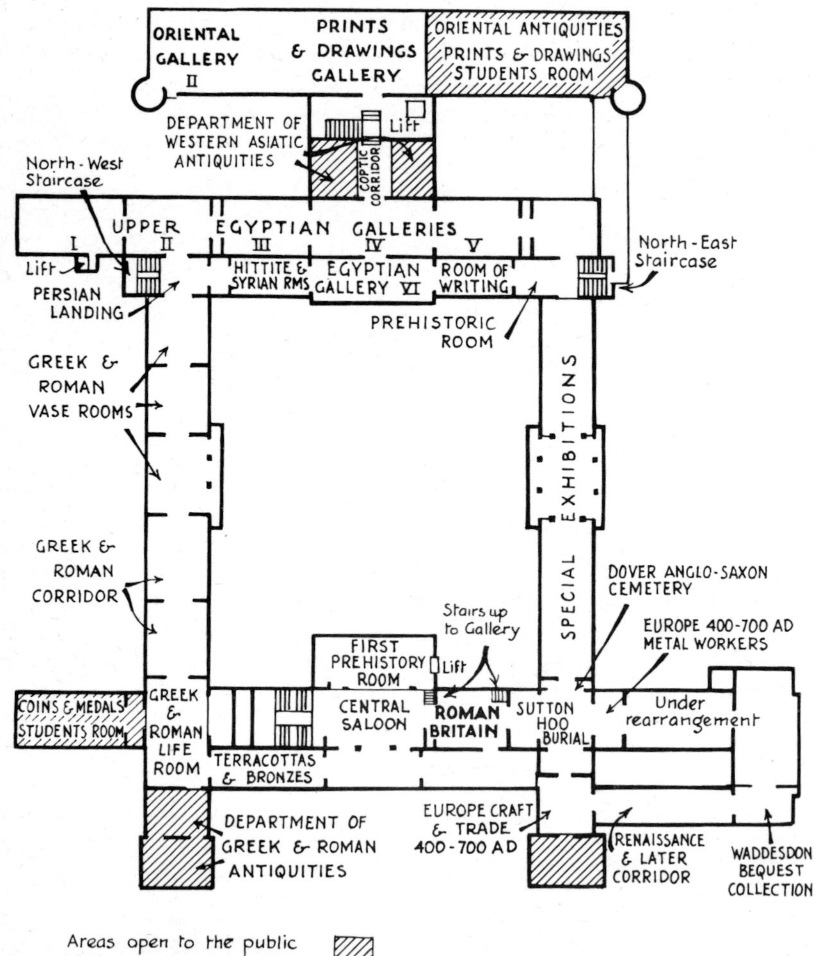

the lay-out of the building is much simpler than its companion in South Kensington. Famous individual items on display include the Elgin Marbles from the Parthenon (the Duveen Gallery), the

Portland Vase (First Roman Room), the Sutton Hoo Treasure (adjoining Roman Britain, Upper Floor) the Rosetta Stone (South Egyptian Gallery), and the Mildenhall treasure (Roman Britain, Upper Floor).

The British Museum also holds a magnificent collection of pictorial art most of it admittedly not on display, but no serious art student will wish to miss the following during a visit. From the Main Entrance turn right off the Front Hall into the Grenville Library which displays a selection of English illuminated manuscripts, including the *Benedictional of St Ethelwold* (Case 1), the *Evesham Psalter* (Case 4), the *Queen Mary Psalter* (Case 6), the *Luttrell Psalter* (Case 8), and the *Bedford Hours and Psalter* (Case 10). The Continental Manuscript cases thereafter have the *Bedford Hours* (Case 6) and the Flemish *Book of Hours* and the *Breviary of Queen Isabella of Spain* (both Case 8). Continue into the Manuscript Saloon where pages from Durer's sketchbook can be seen, and also the incredibly beautiful *Lindisfarne Gospels*, second only to the *Book of Kells* in Dublin as an example of Celtic interlaced ornament. In the first part of the King's Library are six cases featuring a selection of the glories of oriental manuscripts in Arabic, Hebrew and Persian as well as a variety of Indian manuscripts in a number of scripts. The far end of the King's Library has the north eastern staircase leading to the upper floor and the Babylonian Room which adjoins the Upper Egyptian Galleries. Ascend the stairs and walk along to the Fourth Room where you come to the Coptic Corridor on the right. The Coptic Corridor has a small display of portraits painted in the Roman period, remarkable for their technique and freshness alike. The steps at the other end of the Corridor lead to the entrance door of the Prints and Drawings Room. There is no knowing in advance what will be on display here for this room draws upon one of the world's greatest collections of prints and drawings of all the Western movements and schools and that includes Durer, Leonardo, Michelangelo, Rembrandt, and virtually every Old Master one can think of, with Claude, Watteau and Turner very fully represented indeed, to say nothing of the predictably vast holdings of English watercolours which include Blake and Palmer. (To the right of the gallery is the Prints and Drawings Students Room for those who have the time and inclination and have made the necessary prior arrangements to explore the holdings further).

To the left is the Oriental Gallery which similarly shows the iceberg tip of vast holdings on a temporary and changing basis and where one may be treated to displays of Chinese, Japanese, Tibetan, Persian or Indian paintings and illuminations depending on the current arrangements.

The Thomas Coram Foundation for Children: The Foundling Hospital

40 Brunswick Square, W.C.1 (See map p. 64).
Telephone 01–278–1911
Opening Hours Mondays and Fridays only 10.00 to 12.00 and 14.00 to 16.00
Closed At all other times and on Bank Holiday Mondays and Good Friday.
Admission A small charge
Parking Some meters in the area
How to get there **Underground**: Russell Square **Buses**: 68, 77, 77a, 77c, 170, 188, 239.

A continuing testament to a fascinating piece of social history, the Foundling Hospital was founded by Captain Thomas Coram in 1739. The system, as it then operated, was to provide care and protection for children whose mothers were unable to fulfil their normal roles. Children, who might otherwise have been deserted or abandoned in the streets, were brought along to Coram's Foundation where the competition for places was so fierce, they were allocated by ballot. Three billiard balls were placed in a sack, the white ball marked acceptance, the red ball a place on the waiting list, and the white ball with the black spot a refusal. In return for the child, the mother was given a token with which she could later redeem the child if her economic circumstances changed. Coram's close friend William Hogarth, a passionate champion of the underprivileged, was an original member of the Foundation, an example followed later by Hayman, Highmore, Gainsborough, Ramsay, Reynolds and Richard Wilson – and they all donated paintings to the hospital to help it.

From the Inner Hall, climb the stairs (actually the original and beautiful oak staircase of the hospital) to the First Landing which has Hogarth's famous portrait of *Thomas Coram*, a worthy tribute to the powers of both men. Of no particular artistic importance, but an interesting social document of the hospital's work can be seen at the very top of the stairs in four paintings by Emma Brown-King. The main artistic interest, however, remains on the first floor. In the lobby outside the Court Room (to the right off the landing) is Hogarth's canvas *The March of the Guards to Finchley*. Hogarth originally disposed of this picture by lottery and gave some unsold tickets to the hospital – the winning ticket was amongst them. The historical event depicted is the move of the English soldiers recalled to England from Holland to defend the capital against the Jacobite rising in the North. They are at the Tottenham Court Turnpike and whatever military discipline is being showed in the background as the march begins, the foreground teems with the vigorous and indeed dissolute intermingling of soldiers and citizens. Painted by anyone else, we would have had to call it Hogarthian to do it justice.

The Court Room itself, impeccably restored here, has the four biblical pictures, Hogarth's *Moses Brought to Pharoah's Daughter*, Francis Hayman's *Finding of the Infant Moses*, Joseph Highmore's *Hagar and Ishmael* and James Wills' *Little Children Brought to Christ*, all of them subjects chosen with the Foundation in mind. The room also has landscape roundels by Richard Wilson and Gainsborough.

The Picture Gallery (to the left of the staircase) has Millais' *Luther Holden*, Allan Ramsay's *Richard Mead*, Reynolds' *William Legge* and, dwarfing these and the room, a cartoon from Raphael's studio which, unlike those in the V & A, has been overpainted in oils and varnished. Its theme *Massacre of the Innocents* has added point here.

Sir John Soane's Museum

13 Lincoln's Inn Fields, W.C.2. (See map p. 64).
Telephone 01–405–2107
Opening Hours Tuesday to Saturday 10.00 to 17.00
Closed **Mondays, Sundays. Throughout the month of August.** Good Friday, most Bank holidays.
Admission Free.
Parking Some meters in area but often difficult to find a place.
How to get there **Underground:** Holborn. **Buses:** 8, 22, 25, 55,

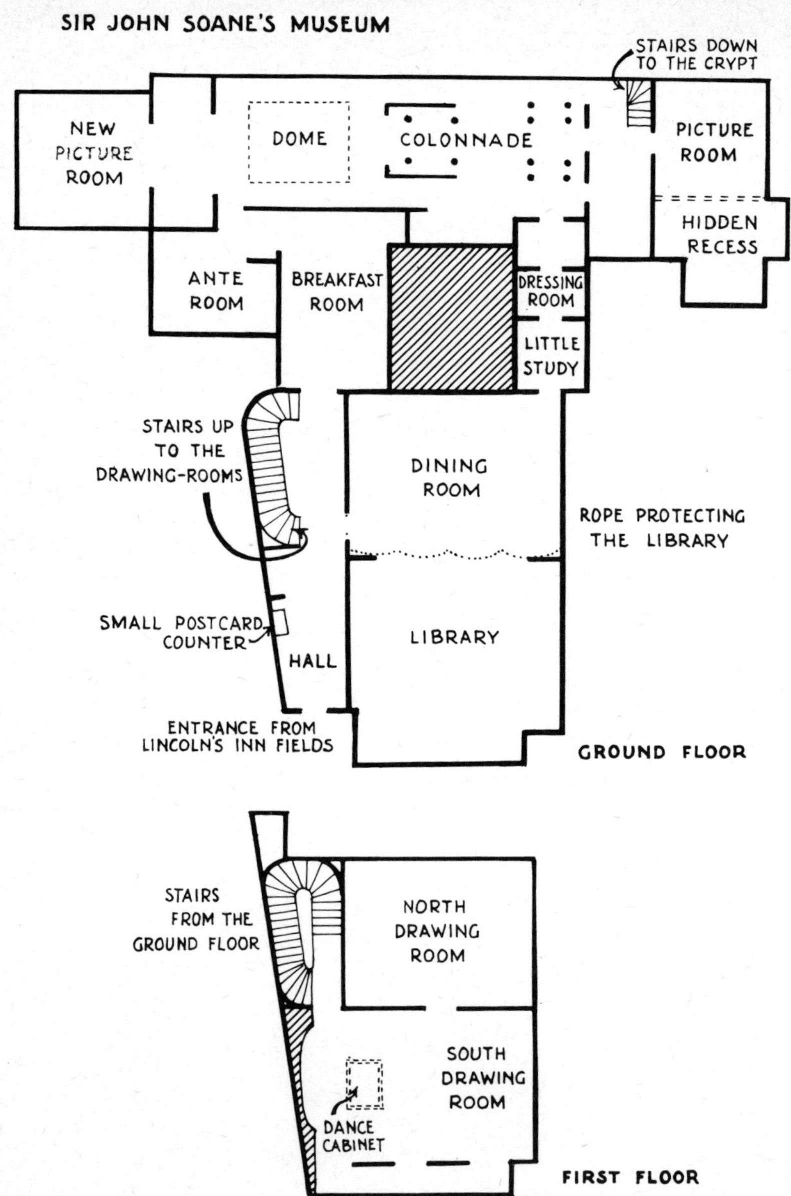
SIR JOHN SOANE'S MUSEUM
STAIRS DOWN TO THE CRYPT
NEW PICTURE ROOM
DOME
COLONNADE
PICTURE ROOM
HIDDEN RECESS
ANTE ROOM
BREAKFAST ROOM
DRESSING ROOM
LITTLE STUDY
STAIRS UP TO THE DRAWING-ROOMS
DINING ROOM
ROPE PROTECTING THE LIBRARY
SMALL POSTCARD COUNTER
LIBRARY
HALL
ENTRANCE FROM LINCOLN'S INN FIELDS
GROUND FLOOR
STAIRS FROM THE GROUND FLOOR
NORTH DRAWING ROOM
SOUTH DRAWING ROOM
DANCE CABINET
FIRST FLOOR

68, 77, 77a, 77c, 170, 188, 239, 501.
Facilities Some postcards for sale in entrance hall.

Other are more impressive, many are larger, most are more exclusive, but Soane's has to be the most eccentric and charming museum in London – a kind of fantasy-cum-junk shop and a total delight. Soane was a neo-classical architect who surrounded himself with architectural bric-a-brac and some remarkably fine pictures and designed a fantastic setting to hold them and him in what must have been impressive discomfort.

Once inside the hall turn right into the Dining Room and Library. The ceiling panels by Henry Howard are far less interesting than the two paintings in the Dining Room area. Over the fireplace is a portrait by Sir Thomas Lawrence of *Sir John Soane*, our eccentric host and subject here of one of Lawrence's finest portraits. Opposite is *Love and Beauty* where Sir Joshua Reynolds has also excelled himself, this time in banality, and in which the half-nude lady peeks at us with one eye and one nipple like some Grand Style plate from an eighteenth century Playgirl calendar. Walk through the tiny Study and Dressing Room and turn right into the Picture Room.

The Picture Room is unexpectedly tiny, but then an attendant will step forward and reveal that the walls are hinged planes and open out into the room to show more pictures underneath and others on the back of the shutters themselves. Furthermore the 'wall' on the right conceals a tall recess packed with topographical, architectural and theatrical drawings and paintings. We must concentrate on those of particular merit. To left and right before the planes are opened are the four works comprising William Hogarth's magnificent *Election Series*. Purchased by Soane at a sale of David Garrick's effects, these superb works are exceptional even for Hogarth for their masterly composition, their splendid handling of paint and colour, and their savage comment upon the electoral system circa 1750. The scene is Oxfordshire. *An Election Entertainment* is thrown by the Whigs where the wine flows in return for votes promised with Hogarth perhaps intending to parody the Last Supper. The two candidates are beneath the flag (left), one nuzzled by an old woman and the other by the drunk at the table. The effigy outside the window is inscribed 'No Jews'. The Mayor (right) has passed out from over-indulgence in oysters.

That such activities are not in accord with true Whig principles can be guessed from the fact that the central portrait on the wall of William III has been slashed through. *Canvassing for Votes* shows the Tory bribing technique in action, and a Tory mob in the background besieging the Crown (the tax-raising Excise authority). In *The Polling* (there was no secret ballot and voting involved a public declaration at the hustings for those who had the courage), the sick, the crippled and even the dead are brought to the poll. Britannia, in her coach, is allegorically overturned by such goings-on. *Chairing the Member* shows the victory procession with the winner (he looks remarkably like George Bubb Dodington, whose surviving diary tells us much of the political wheeling-dealing of the times) held aloft, a symbolic goose flying overhead, and fleeing pigs dashing off like Gadarene swine to the accompaniment of the syphilitic fiddler (right).

To accompany this masterly series is yet another – the even more famous *Rake's Progress*, all eight reading from left to right as follows, *The Young Heir taking Possession* (Tom Rakewell the heir is measured for a mourning suit for his father's funeral); *The Levee* (Tom holds court to the hangers-on, musicians, fencing masters etc); *The Orgy* (The Rose Tavern, Covent Garden and Tom petted and robbed simultaneously); *The Arrest* (Tom arrested for debt in St James's Street); *The Marriage* (Tom marries a one-eyed widow for her fortune as Sarah, the mother of his illegitimate child, is prevented from entering the church to stop the ceremony); *The Gambling House* (The widow's fortune has found its way into the pockets of knaves and gamblers); *The Prison* (Tom in prison for debt, taunted by his wife while the faithful Sarah swoons at his initial signs of insanity); and *The Mad-house* (Tom in Bedlam asylum, a sort of tourist attraction for the aristocracy who can watch the victims of delusion enact their fantasies. Only Sarah has any sympathy for him).

When these series have been digested look also for the Turner *Kirkstall Abbey* watercolour, Francis Danby's *Merchant of Venice Scene* (behind the left-hand plane); Thornhill's *Sketch for Queen's Bed Chamber, Hampton Court* (above the *Rake's Progress*); and Fuseli's *Count of Ravenna musing over Meduna slain by him for Infidelity during his absence in the Holy Land* (left of the doorway).

From the Picture Room, the New Picture Room is reached by

walking through the Colonnade and under the Dome. It contains Turner's *Admiral Tromp's Barge,* and Canaletto's three Venetian scenes *The Grand Canal, Piazza San Marco,* and *The Rialto.*

The South Drawing Room on the first floor has Reynolds' Italian Sketchbook in a case on the table in the middle of the room, and over the fireplace in the North Drawing Room next door, hangs Watteau's *Les Noces.*

The Courtauld Institute Galleries

The Courtauld-Warburg Building, Woburn Square, W.C.1. (See map p. 64).

Telephone 01–580–1015 or 01–636–2095

Opening Hours Monday to Saturday 10.00 to 17.00 (including Bank Holiday Mondays) Sunday 14.00 to 17.00

Closed Good Friday, Christmas Eve, Christmas Day, Boxing Day, New Year's Day.

Admission Free

Parking Some meters in area so a matter of luck.

How to get there **Underground:** Goodge Street, Euston Square, Russell Square. **Buses:** 68, 77, 77a, 77c, 170, 188, 239 get off at Woburn Place; 14, 24, 29, 73, 176, to Gower Street (if going south) and get off at Torrington Place near Dillon's Bookshop; or Tottenham Court Road (if going north) and get off at Goodge Street.

Not much more than five minutes walk away from the north entrance of the British Museum, yet visited by only a fraction of the millions who pound the BM's many rooms, the Courtauld galleries are perhaps my personal favourite among London's galleries. Small enough to be reasonably embraced at one sitting, its rare collection can be seen in a luxurious sofa'd and carpetted comfort unrivalled among its competitors. The unassuming entrance is not easily seen from a distance, and the lift which takes one from the ground floor to the galleries themselves is a misleading overture for the pleasure to come. The paintings incidentally are not covered with glass so one can view without the maddening distraction of reflections.

The first room, Room IA, has some rare early works so do not miss them in your eagerness to pass on to the better known Old and Modern masters. Simone Martini is probably responsible for

The Crucified Christ; Noli Me Tangere comes from a follower of Giotto; *St Catherine of Bologna* herself a miniaturist is the quaint central figure in the panel by the Master of Baroncelli Portraits. The large *'Estouteville Triptych'* is believed to be fourteenth century English (the left wing shows the Annunciation, the Magi, and the Presentation, and the right wing the Ascension, Pentecost, and Dormition of the Virgin). Look next at the German early fifteenth century *Crucifixion* with the large expressive almost expressionist heads and the odd iconography – the crucified thief on the left has his soul (the small figure coming out of his mouth) received by angelic hands, but the one on the right, perhaps the bad thief, has his seized by a small demon. Look too, if you can bear it, at the realism of the wounds of all three. Room IB is a natural extension of IA and has *The Nativity and Adoration of the Magi* by the Master of the Gambier-Parry Nativity (of Rimini), Martino di Bartolommeo of Siena's *Madonna and Child,* a case of ivory diptychs and triptychs on the left hand wall, a Florentine *Annunciation* (known I wonder to Crivelli later?) a Leonardoesque *Annunciation* by Pesellino and a Botticellilike *Virgin and Child* by the Master of San Miniato. The case on the right hand wall includes pages from an illuminated Book of Hours from c. 1415 and rich in decoration. IC continues with Lorenzo Monaco's *Visitation* and its pair *The Adoration of Kings.*

Room II is similarly rich in early work. Bernardo Daddi's Florentine tempera and tooled gilt *Polyptych*, an excellent example of the continuing influence of Giotto, features (from left to right) Saints Lawrence, Andrew, Bartholomew, and George to the left of the central Crucifixion, and Saints Paul, Peter, James the Great, and Stephen on the right hand panels. Don't miss on the right hand wall, Mariotto Albertinelli's *The Creation* which is stylistically close to Piero di Cosimo and combines successive episodes in the story like a strip cartoon. Eve rises curiously from Adam's side, like Esther Williams from a swimming pool. The case of maiolica ware nearby is also a delight.

Room III has the Lee Collection. Here is a Rubens study for *The Descent from the Cross* with a dynamic diagonal sweep to the composition adding to the drama, and a characteristically athletic torso for Christ. Van Dyck's *Christ on the Cross* is by contrast the loneliest man in the world against the blue night sky. Notice that the brown and white border is painted. At the end of the room is the large Botticelli *Holy Trinity*. The colouring is very Florentine, God the Father is particularly benign, surrounded as He is with healthy cherubs, John the Baptist stands right and Mary Magdalene left though she looks very masculine, and the tiny figures in the foreground are Tobias and the Angel – their diminutive stature probably explained by their relative theological unimportance. Further along is the *Assassination of St Peter Martyr*, attributed to Bellini and comparable to a similar larger version in the National Gallery though note that here the tree stumps give out blood. In Bernardo Luini's *Madonna and Child* note the qualities imparted by the Holy Spirit are labelled on the rays around the dove, and that the figure on the right who empties his purse to the kneeling beggar is St Antonius, Archbishop of Florence. Lucas Cranach the Elder's *Adam and Eve* are distinctly erotic, with the vine leaves strategically placed to hide their sexual characteristics serving more to emphasise than conceal, and the pink apples looking all too edible. The attendant animals and birds are particularly charming.

In Room IV, see Romney's *Georgiana, Lady Greville*, Goya's *Don Francisco de Saavedra* and Gainsborough's *The Artist's Wife* (a brilliant exercise in careful 'careless' brushstrokes, and a sitter of warmth and dignity).

Rooms V and VI feature the Courtauld collection itself, an eminently distinguished selection of French paintings of the nineteenth century. V has Daumier's *Don Quixote and Sancho Panza* where the paint is applied so thinly it actually drips, and the canvas ground shows through. The literary figures themselves have become almost abstract particularly about the head. Degas' *Two Dancers* is the subject of a moment, Cezanne's *Still-life with Plaster Cast* almost of an eternity. Then we come to one of the world's most famous pictures Manet's *Bar at the Folies-Bergère*, his last work and a solid and unchallengeable masterpiece. The barmaid and her customer are reflected in the mirror behind her as is the scene in the theatre. Manet signed the picture on the label of the red bottle on the left, and look how cunningly he emphasises the arbitrary nature of the composition by the pale green legs in the top left hand corner (they belong to an otherwise unseen trapeze artist). Also here are Sisley's *Snow at Louveciennes*, Degas' pastel *Woman Drying Herself*, Pissarro's *Penge Station* (not as surprising a subject as one might first imagine, for the Frenchman was once a South London refugee from the Franco-Prussian War), Renoir's *La Loge* (surely the hand holding the opera glasses is a poor piece of drawing?) and a group of Cezanne's including one version of *The Card Players*, one version of *Montagne Sainte Victoire, Man Smoking a Pipe* and *Lake of Annecy*. The other Manet, *Le Dejeuner sur l'Herbe*, is a slightly smaller version of the work now in the Louvre which created a sensation in Paris at the 1863 Salon. The figures are exactly as they are in the Louvre picture except that the faces are little more than suggested.

Room VI continues at the same high level with Seurat's *Young Woman with a powder-puff* (the mirror on the wall is believed once to have contained a Seurat self-portrait which got painted out later) and also his *Bridge at Courbevois*. Note that Seurat carries his colour theories to the extent of painting a special border around his work – the one around the powder-puff painting is predominantly blue at the base but gets more red towards the top, and naturally affects the colour values of the work itself. Dufy's *Sailing Boat* and Rousseau's *Customs House* (of the painter's own workplace) lead to another famous canvas – Vincent Van Gogh's *Portrait of the Artist with bandaged ear* painted after Van Gogh had physically attacked Gauguin and then turned his violent tendencies upon himself, severing his own ear from his head with a razor. Look how the colours anticipate the Fauves – the green eyes and the red and green shadows on the face, and the use of Prussian Blue straight from the tube to lift the coat and hat from the pale lemon background – and how they illuminate the state of mind of this desperate man. In his *Peach Trees in Blossom* nearby, the colour is quieter but the paint applied very thickly and virtually encrusted on the canvas. Gauguin, Van Gogh's one-time friend and painting companion, also uses blue lines sometimes to define forms. In *Te Rerioa* ('Day-dreaming'), the blue lines enclose, for example, the loincloth and toes of the right-hand figure – whose head incidentally seems not entirely accurately placed on her shoulders. Perhaps that is why the other girl smiles smugly. Toulouse-Lautrec's *Tête-à-Tête Supper* has a whore with a cupid-bow mouth to outdo Bette Davis – her supper companion may be the English painter Charles Conder. Bonnard's *Blue Balcony* leads to some more Gauguins – *Haystacks* and one, *Nevermore*, which pays deliberate homage to

Manet's *Olympia* (in the Louvre), but not to Edgar Allen Poe as the title and the raven on the sill suggests. Gauguin once said the work was badly painted but the satisfactory way the girl's dark hair and brown flesh complement the creamy-yellow pillow makes him too modest. The alcoholic Utrillo's *Street at Sannois* precedes Toulouse-Lautrec's *Jane Avril*, with one eye closed and the other more mascara than anything else, and which is not gouache as might be thought at first glance, but in fact one of the finest pastels one could imagine. Monet's *Antibes* is also here.

Room VIII, when not occupied by special exhibitions, has work from France and England, collected by Roger Fry, naturally including work by the local artists – the Bloomsbury Group, together with items from his Omega workshop and Modigliani's erotic *Nude*. Room VIII sometimes shows selections from the Witt collection of drawings.

In a Hurry The Galleries in their entirety can be covered in 15 or 20 minutes but if you really have to make a flying visit make sure you see the *Estouteville Triptych* in IA; Daddi's *Polyptych* in II; Botticelli's *Holy Trinity* in III; Gainsborough's *The Artist's Wife* in IV; Manet's *Bar at the Folies-Bergère*, Cezanne's *Montagne Sainte Victoire*, Manet's *Dejeuner sur l'Herbe* study all in V; and in VI Van Gogh's *Portrait of the Artist with Bandaged Ear*, Gauguin's *Te Rerioa* and *Nevermore*, and Toulouse-Lautrec's *Jane Avril*. Not, one must say, a bad first eleven.

The Wallace Collection

Manchester Square, W.1. (See map p.78).
Telephone 01–935–0687
Opening Hours Monday to Saturday 10.00 to 17.00. Sunday 14.00 to 17.00.
Closed Good Friday, Christmas Eve, Christmas Day, Boxing Day, New Year's Day.
Admission Free
Parking Forbidden in the forecourt, some meters and some commercial parks in the vicinity.
How to get there **Underground:** Bond Street. **Buses:** 1, 2, 2b, 13, 26, 30, 59, 74, 74b, 113, 159 and get off at Portman Square, 6, 7, 8, 12, 15, 73, 88, 137, 500, 505, 616 to Oxford Street and get off

at Selfridge's.

Facilities Postcard and catalogue counter in entrance hall. Free lectures usually at 13.00 on Wednesdays and 14.30 on Fridays but check with the collection for details.

One of the world's most valuable collections of furniture, ornaments, porcelain, armour and paintings, the Wallace is, or should be, a must on anyone's list of priority visits. Nowhere outside France is eighteenth century French art better represented, and indeed even a visitor from France would need to see some of its glories to supplement the holdings in his own country. The paintings are enhanced by the charm of the setting, with elegant furniture and ornaments, and the ticking of ormolu clocks.

The entrance hall contains Sir Thomas Lawrence's *King George IV*. To the right are Rooms I and II which can be treated as one. They have *An unknown lady* by Lawrence; the suicidal Le Moine's *Time Revealing Truth*, Van Loo's *King Louis XV* and two Oudry still-life and dog paintings far above the normal standards of the

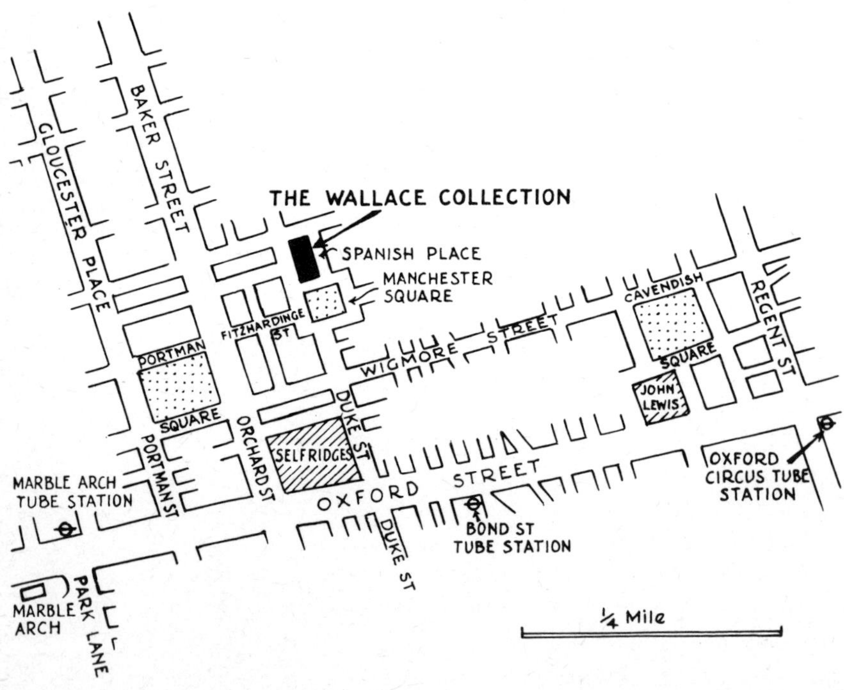

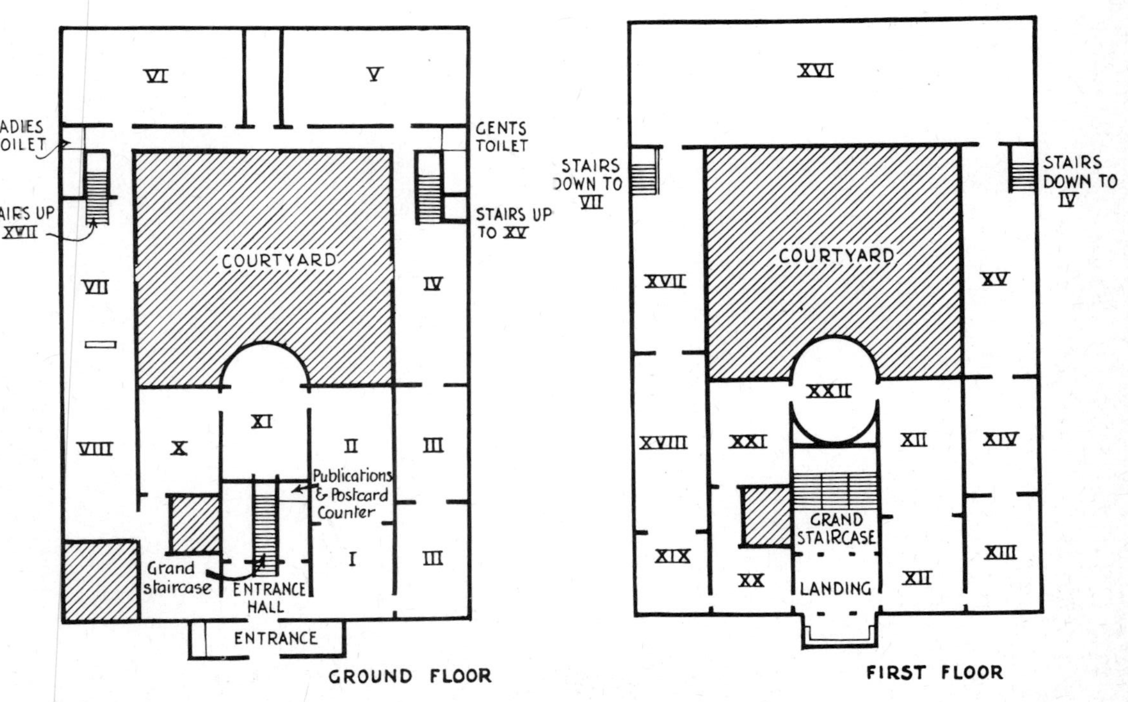
THE WALLACE COLLECTION
VI
V
LADIES TOILET
GENTS TOILET
STAIRS UP TO XVII
STAIRS UP TO XV
COURTYARD
VII
IV
XI
VIII
X
II
III
Publications & Postcard Counter
Grand staircase
ENTRANCE HALL
I
III
ENTRANCE
GROUND FLOOR
XVI
STAIRS DOWN TO VII
STAIRS DOWN TO IV
COURTYARD
XVII
XV
XXII
XVIII
XXI
XII
XIV
GRAND STAIRCASE
XIX
XX
LANDING
XII
XIII
FIRST FLOOR

genre – *The Dead Wolf* and *The Dead Roe*. At the right of the fireplace turn left into Room III and see the fragments from Italian illuminated manuscripts of the fourteenth and fifteenth centuries in the third glass case in the middle of the room. Do not move on till you have seen also Crivelli's *St Roch* and Memlinc's *St Michael* to the sides of the doorway to IV, and especially the Bronzino portrait of *Eleonora di Toledo* in the corner opposite the entrance from I and II. IV has the very fine Philippe de Champaigne *Adoration of the Shepherds* on the right hand wall but its effects are badly hampered by the reflections from the glass covering its surface.

From IV, the emphasis is temporarily on armour with V, VI and VII devoted to European armour, and VIII to oriental arms and armour. Continue walking until you see another doorway on the left leading into IX where a portrait of *George III* by Allan Ramsay, and Venetian landscapes by Canaletto and Guardi hang. The Corridor leading into X has Bonington water-colours on the left hand wall and Turner watercolours on the right.

In X itself, we are in Northern Italy and its various schools. Over the chimney-piece is the altarpiece *Mystic Marriage of Saint Catherine* by Sassoferrato and the room has, among others, *Venus and Cupid* perhaps by Titian, Andrea del Sarto's *Virgin and Child with John the Baptist*, and an important central panel from a Cima altarpiece of *St Catherine of Alexandria* (who is unlikely to have been authentic despite having given her name to the Catherine wheel). See here also Vannuccio's *Virgin and Child with Saints* a fourteenth century work of fine quality.

XI is mainly distinguished by the works of Murillo and his followers. He himself has five religious pieces here, *Virgin in Glory, Marriage of the Virgin, Charity of Saint Thomas* (over the fireplace) and, to the left and right, *Adoration of the Shepherds* and *Joseph and his Brethren*. The octagonal case has Napoleonic miniatures, and the two upright cases by the windows, a number of other miniatures including Hans Holbein the Younger's *Self-portrait*. The other doorway from XI returns us to Rooms II and I for us to take the door on the right back into the entrance hall.

We must now mount the very grand Grand Staircase – of marble with a forced bronze and iron, chased and gilt balustrade. If you cannot see the two Boucher canvasses *Rising and Setting of*

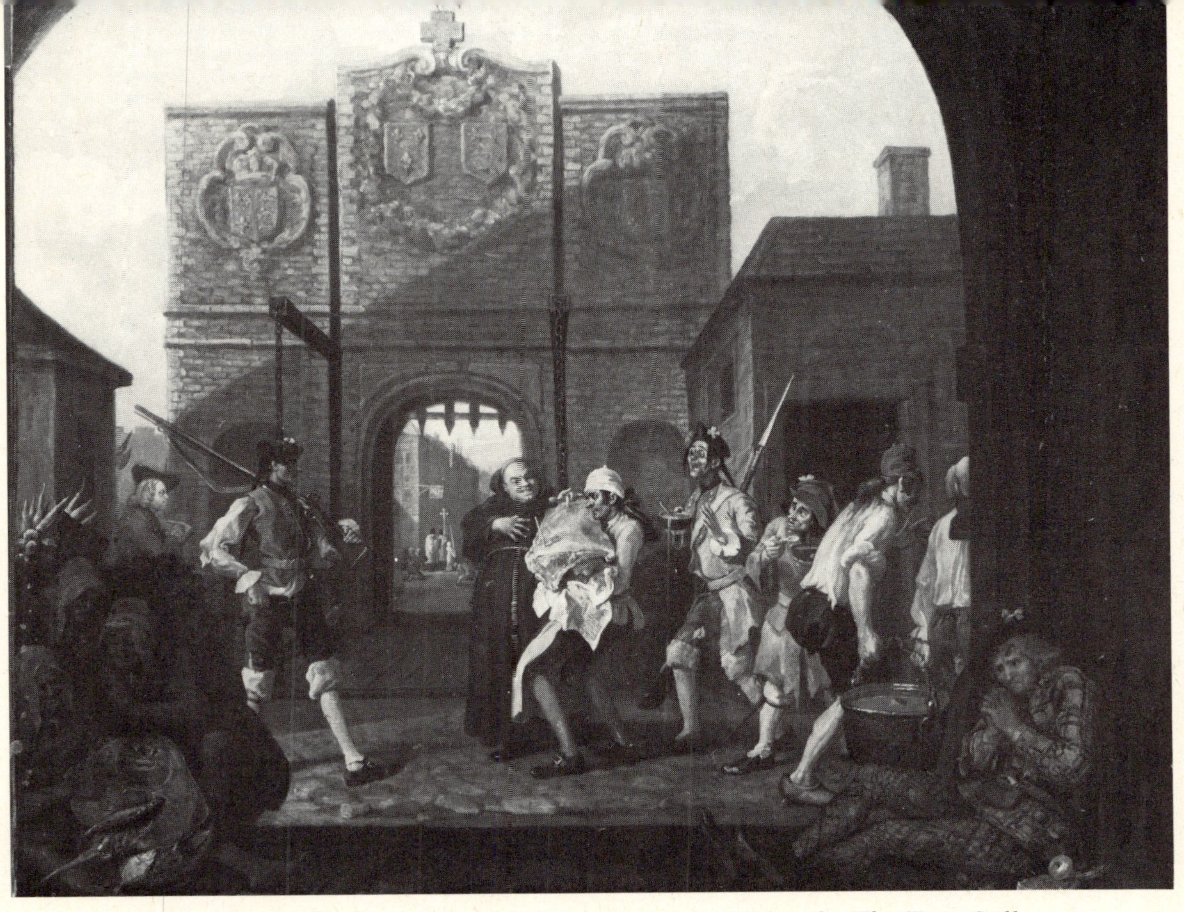

The Roast Beef of Old England ('Calais Gate') by Hogarth, *The Tate Gallery*

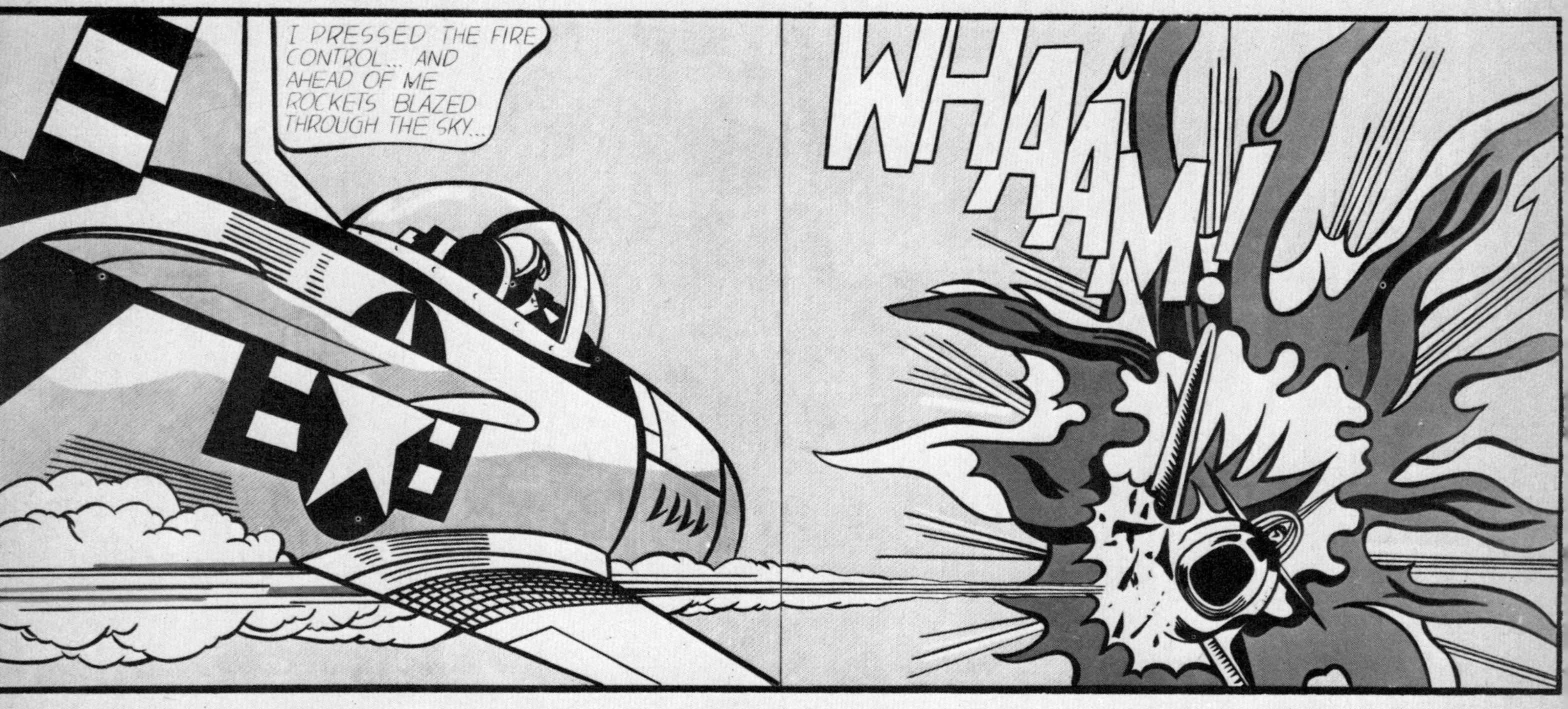

Whaam! by Roy Lichtenstein, *The Tate Gallery*

the Sun because of the reflections, look again when you reach the balcony and landing. The small Conservatory here also offers a good opportunity for a sit down before continuing our tour. With the stairs at your back turn left into XII. XII has four large Guardis of Venice – *Santa Maria della Salute, The Rialto, San Giorgio Maggiore*, and *The Dogana* – as well as some smaller ones, and Guardi's mentor Canaletto graces the right-hand wall with two paintings of *The Bacino di San Marco* and another of the *Fete on the Piazzetta*. At the south end of the room, a door to the left leads to XIII. This has a number of Rubens sketches including *Adoration of the Magi* and above them on the wall his *Christ on the Cross* with its bulging tortured arms. Rembrandt's *Good Samaritan* and his own etching of the subject are also here. Pass on into the next room XIV, mostly devoted to Dutch seventeenth century genre works including Jan Steen's *Harpsichord Lesson*, Gabriel Metsu's *The Letter Writer Surprised*, Esaias Boursse's *Interior with Woman Cooking*, Steen's *Village Alchemist* and Nicholas Maes' *The Listening Housewife*; while the next room XV is of Dutch landscapes and seascapes of the same period – van Ruisdael's *Landscape with Farm*, Hobbema's *Landscape with Watermill* and *Ruin on the Banks of a River*, paintings by both older and younger Van der Veldes, and Cuyp's *The Avenue at Meerdervoort*.

Room XVI is the largest room in the house. It is also one of the choicest selections of masterpieces anywhere in the world – a room offering genius cheek by jowl with genius – a place to wonder at, to admire and to return to again and again. A rare Reynolds religious picture *St John in the Wilderness* and a Titian-like Van Dyck *The Shepherd Paris* (in fact a handsome self-portrait) are followed by a brilliant Reynolds portrait *Nelly O'Brien*, a Watteau much larger than usual in *The Halt During the Chase* and another Reynolds of *Mrs Hoare and her son*. An authentic Titian, painted by him when in full possession of his powers is the superb *Perseus and Andromeda* where Perseus takes a headlong fall, and Andromeda is a beautifully painted nude. Gainsborough in *Miss Haverfield* shows that Reynolds does not have child portraiture to himself. Watteau's charming *Fête in a park* almost conceals the weakness of its draughtsmanship. Rubens' *Isabella Brant* is actually his first wife with the truthful painter perhaps triumphing over the husband's desire to flatter.

Register the Velazquez *Don Baltasar Carlos* on horseback and pass on to his famous and brilliant *Lady with a Fan* once belonging to the Bonaparte family, and so fresh and vibrant it might have been painted yesterday. The puzzling *Allegorical Love-feast* by Pieter Pourbus has some puzzling sexual overtones but its meanings escape me despite the helpful labelling of the personae on their sleeves and waistbands. Another Velazquez *Don Baltasar Carlos* which follows shows him in infancy (actually he died aged 17).

Another masterly portraitist, Rembrandt, makes his appearance on the westerly end wall with *Jean Pellicorne with his son Gaspar*. Rubens turns his attention to religion with the magnificent *Holy Family with Saints Elizabeth and John the Baptist*, and although Jacob Jordaens' important *Riches of Autumn* is difficult to see for reflections on the glass, Rubens continues in the same magnificent vein with *Christ's Charge to Peter*. The other end of the wall has another Rembrandt group, *Susanna van Collen and her daughter*.

The long northern wall is as festooned with great works as the others if not more so. Rembrandt extends his vision to himself with *The Artist in a Cap* and another seventeenth century Dutchman Albert Cuyp shows up with *River Scene with view of Dordrecht*. Reynolds, not to be outdone, produces *The Strawberry Girl* and the full-length *Mrs Carnac*. Pieter de Hoogh's intimate *Woman Peeling Apples* takes us on to another Rubens, arguably the finest painting in the entire rich collection – *The Rainbow Landscape*, a kind of unique blend of the vigour one associates with youth and the mature contemplation of nature of the middle-aged or elderly, and carried out not for a patron but for his own pleasure. Look at the handling of the rainbow itself, of the light glancing on the tops of the trees, and of the tiny splashes of colour on the ducks in the right hand corner – and you will see why Rubens was such a great technician. And having digested the glories of Rubens and Van Dyck's *Marie de Raet*, there is another Rembrandt to give you goose-pimples too – the portrait of his son *Titus* (Titus was his son by Saskia) at about the age of 16. Compare it with the similar one in Dulwich (see p. 94-5) when Titus was older. Of the two I find the Wallace one the more profound. We continue with Jacob van Ruisdael's *Rocky Landscape* and Domenichino's *The Persian Sibyl* (in an exotic turban and odd sleeves, one red and one blue) leading to one of Salvator Rosa's greatest works *Landscape with Apollo*, and his *The Cumaean Sibyl* (actually the figures are unimportant and are dwarfed by the romantic landscape). Next is another of the world's most famous paintings, *The Laughing Cavalier* by Frans Hals – full of inspired brushwork but, for me, also intolerably full of self-satisfied bourgeois smugness. Painter and sitter alike seem too clever for their own good. After it, Hobbema's *Stormy Landscape* and even Reynolds' *Miss Jane Bowles*, in which the child likes posing as much as the dog does not, come as a relief. How confident males *should* be painted is demonstrated in the imposing and masterly *Philippe Le Roy* by Van Dyck. (The sitter was the husband of the Marie de Raet we saw previously). More religious works follow in the shape of Rembrandt's *Centurion Cornelius* (Cornelius was sent to Peter after a visitation from an angel – see Acts X 1–48) and over on the end wall, Murillo's *Holy Family with Saint John the Baptist* with its soft limpid colour. Poussin's *Dance to the Music of Time* is succeeded by the colossal *Annunciation* by Philippe de Champaigne, the French artist who collaborated with the young Poussin in decorating the Luxembourg in the early part of his career but later turned to the severe Jansenist sect and devoted himself strictly to religious works. Claude's *Italian landscape* and another Murillo *The Annunciation* brings us to the close of this room which could hardly be worth more money if it was covered from floor to ceiling in gold bars.

Room XVII is inevitably an anti-climax but look at Delacroix's *Execution of Doge Marino Faliero*, Meissonier's *An Artist Showing his work* (the surface is cracking), and Corot's *Macbeth and the Witches* (dominated by dark trees and sombre skies). XVIII is a celebration of the French eighteenth century, that fragile, sophisticated and dainty world to be swept away by the upheavals of the Revolution of 1789, and represented here by all the names one would expect. A group of Bouchers includes *A Shepherd Watching a Sleeping Shepherdess* (the eroticism of title and picture is deliberate) the Watteaus include *Music Party*, and Watteau's follower, Lancret has *Mademoiselle Carmargo Dancing* among others, and a wide range of Fragonards includes *Fountain of Love, Gardens of The Villa d'Este Tivoli, A Young Scholar*, and *The Souvenir*, leading to his most celebrated work and indeed one of the most celebrated in the entire collection – *The Swing*. This delicately painted incident between man and mistress with the man looking up her dress is full of sexuality, but surely if her knee is where Fragonard places it, there is no way her little bottom can be on the seat of the swing? Greuze's *A Lady* and *Mademoiselle Sophie Arnould,* and Watteau's *Les Champs Elysees* are all in this room too.

XIX specialises in Boucher and includes his most famous portrait, *Madame de Pompadour.* XX on the other hand is dominated by the Englishman Richard Parkes Bonington, with *Sea-piece* (perhaps the best), *Piazza San Marco*, *Coast of Picardy*, and some of his history subjects including *Henri III and the English Ambassador.* His *Sunset in the Pays de Caux* is outside in the Corridor.

The last two rooms are XXI with Lancret's *Italian Comedians by a Fountain* above the veneered cabinet, and XXII with a number of Paters and Greuzes, including the latter's *Votive offering to Cupid.* From XXII move into XII turning right and right again to return to the Grand Staircase, then walk downstairs to the Entrance Hall.

In a hurry

Go straight up the Grand Staircase and turn left into XII to see Canaletto's two versions of *The Bacino di San Marco* and his *Fete on the Piazetta.* Return to the south end of XII and turn left into XIII. Walk through XIII, XIV, and XV into XVI. In XVI see as many works as time permits but especially Reynolds' *Nelly O'Brien,* Watteau's *Halt During the Chase,* Titian's *Perseus and Andromeda*, Velazquez's *Lady with a Fan*, Rubens' *Holy Family* and *Rainbow Landscape*, Rembrandt's *Titus*, Frans Hals' *Laughing Cavalier* and Philippe de Champaigne's *Annunciation.* Take the other exit from XVI and walk through XVII into XVIII for Watteau's *Music Party* and Fragonard's *The Swing.* Go into XIX and straight through XX and you are back on the staircase landing.

6
FURTHER AFIELD

The Imperial War Museum ✓

Lambeth Road, S.E.1. (See map p.88)
Telephone 01–735–8922
Opening Hours Monday to Saturday 10.00 to 18.00 and Sunday 14.00 to 18.00
Closed Good Friday, Christmas Eve, Christmas Day, Boxing Day and New Year's Day.
Admission Free.
Parking Possible in nearby streets.
How to get there **Underground**: Lambeth North, Elephant and Castle. **Buses**: 3, 10a, 44, 59, 109, 155, 159, 172.
Facilities 'Old Bill's' self-service cafeteria on lower floor. Postcard, poster, and booklets counter.

Quite apart from its displays of the technology, sociology and memorabilia of two World Wars, the Museum holds a moving testimony to the effects of military conflict upon some of the most sensitive observers of those troubled times – the artists. It has over 9,000 works taking the First World War as their subject, and a very large percentage of the work produced during the Second World War at the behest of the War Artist's Advisory Committee. With most visitors more interested in the guns, tanks, and aircraft beautifully and imaginatively displayed in most of its galleries, it would be quite impossible to display all the paintings and drawings at once although the Keeper of Pictures will sympathetically consider a request, giving reasonable notice, to view a specific work. Nevertheless, the cream is usually on view, primarily in rooms 3 to 7, though subject to change and re-arrangement from time to time.

A visit to see the paintings should encompass the following: Augustus John's *Lawrence of Arabia* and *Fraternity*, Paul Nash's *Ypres Salient at Night* and many others, Bernard Meninsky's *Victoria Station*, H.S. Williamson's *German Attack*, Leslie Cole's *Naval Base Dentistry*, Anthony Gross' *Battle of Rathedaung* (very good), John Worsley's *Contents of a Red Cross Parcel* (a clever and ingenious still-life), Doris Zinkeisen's horrifying *Belsen*, L.S. Lowry's *Going to Work*, John Nash's *Dockyard Fire* and *Oppy Wood*, Henry Carr's *Liberation* (a dramatic and moving image), Colin Gill's Spencer-like *Heavy Artillery*, C.R.W. Nevinson's

Harvest of Battle, The Road from Arras to Bapaume and others, a brilliant painting by Henry Lamb of *Irish Troops in the Judaean Hills* and Stanley Spencer's *Shipbuilding on the Clyde* panels.

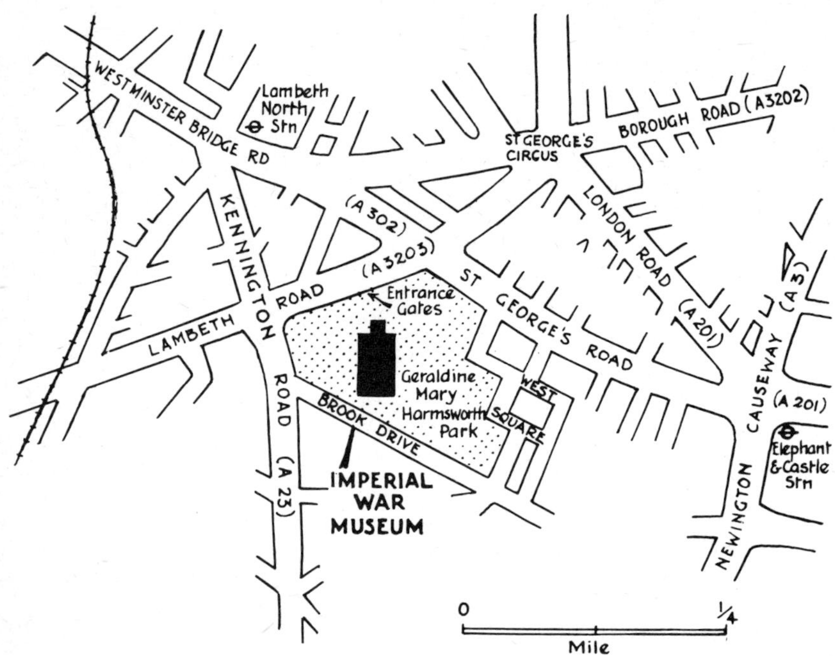

The Henry Lamb in particular serves to emphasise how the extremity of war can sometimes force a minor painter to find powers within himself that in times of peace might have remained untapped. And the point is remade when you pass into room 6 at the entrance to the cinema and see Sargent's huge *Gassed*, a dramatic, brilliant and emotional composition and an incredible contrast to the fashionable drawing-room portraits that were his normal stock-in-trade. Only here, one feels, were his magnificent talents used to full advantage. Also in 6 are usually William Orpen's bland *Peace Conference*, and three other works never surpassed by their painters – *The Underworld* by Walter Bayes, *A Shell Dump, France* by William Roberts (and I do not mean to undervalue his other works), and Charles Sims' *The Old German Front Line*.

On a smaller scale, Room 7 usually has watercolours by Sargent,

Roberts, Orpen, Nevinson and the Nashes among others.

The Hayward Gallery ✓

South Bank, S.E.1. *(Close to the southern end of Waterloo Bridge).*
Telephone 01–928–3144.
Opening Hours During special exhibitions only but then Monday to Friday 10.00 to 20.00, Saturday 10.00 to 18.00, and Sunday 12.00 to 18.00.
Admission charge depending on the scope of the current exhibition.
Parking commercial car parks only
How to get there **Mainline stations**: Waterloo, Charing Cross. **Underground**: Waterloo, Charing Cross. **Buses**: 1, 1a, 4, 68, 70, 76, 149, 168a, 171, 176, 188, 239, 501, 502, 503, 505, 507, 513.

Leased by the Arts Council of Great Britain for major exhibitions, which can range in theme and period from Salvator Rosa or Van Gogh, to Op or Minimal art, the Hayward Gallery has to be one of the ugliest modern buildings in London – not that the competition is anything but fierce – with its grim and windowless concrete exterior soaking up moisture on a wet day like a roll of kitchen paper, and the neon tubes on the roof suggesting a night club. The interior is much preferable, for it has sufficient space on its two floors for adequate display of the largest canvasses, but even there the unfinished concrete seems ungracious. Check with the daily press for details of temporary exhibitions.

A Trip to Hampstead (i) Fenton House

Hampstead Grove, N.W.3. (See map p.90).
Telephone 01–435–3471.
Opening Hours Monday, and Wednesday to Saturday 11.00 to 17.00 or dusk. Sunday from 14.00 to 17.00 or dusk.
Closed **Tuesdays**, Christmas Day, Boxing Day, New Year's Day.
Admission charge.
Parking possible in the streets nearby.
How to get there **Underground**: Hampstead. **Busess**: 210, 268.

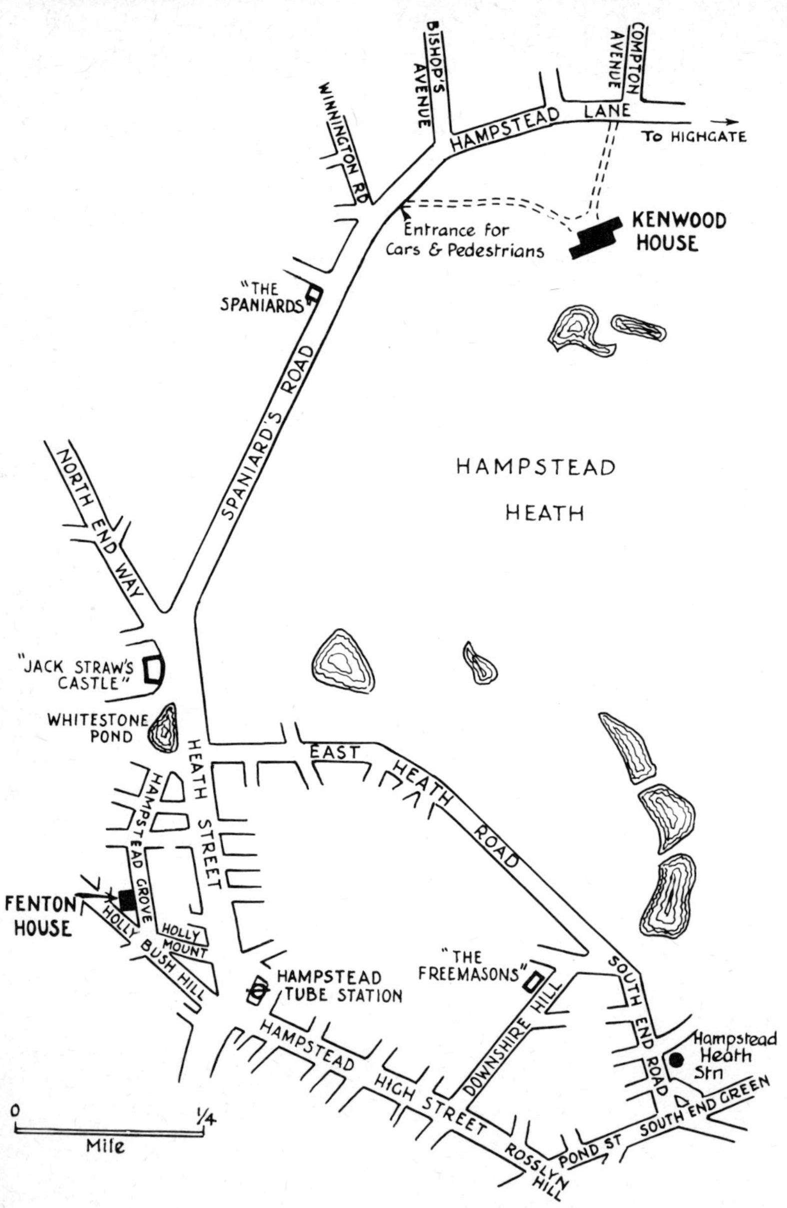
BISHOP'S AVENUE
COMPTON AVENUE
WINNINGTON RD
HAMPSTEAD LANE
To HIGHGATE
Entrance for Cars & Pedestrians
KENWOOD HOUSE
"THE SPANIARDS"
SPANIARD'S ROAD
NORTH END WAY
HAMPSTEAD HEATH
"JACK STRAW'S CASTLE"
WHITESTONE POND
HEATH STREET
EAST HEATH ROAD
HAMPSTEAD GROVE
FENTON HOUSE
HOLLY BUSH HILL
HOLLY MOUNT
HAMPSTEAD TUBE STATION
"THE FREEMASONS"
DOWNSHIRE HILL
SOUTH END ROAD
Hampstead Heath Stn
SOUTH END GREEN
HAMPSTEAD HIGH STREET
ROSSLYN HILL
POND ST
0
1/4
Mile

This late seventeenth century house is one of the most exquisite in London. Not only does it hold an outstanding private collection of all kinds of eighteenth century porcelain, but it also has a remarkable collection of early keyboard instruments so that it is often possible to move from one elegant room to another to the stately sounds of a harpsichord, for the National Trust follows the enlightened practice of allowing music students to play the instruments during opening hours. The house holds very few pictures but they are considerably enhanced by their aural and visual setting. The ground floor Drawing Room has *St Christopher and the Infant Christ* by Adriaen Isenbrant of the Early Netherlandish school at Bruges, *Hampstead Heath under a Stormy Sky* by Constable (Constable once lived in Hampstead, painted many views of the Heath, and is buried in the south east corner of the Hampstead Parish Church a third of a mile from Fenton House), and a moderately large Stubbs. On the first floor, the Blue Porcelain Room has two Paul Sandby landscape watercolours, and the Brown Room has a Durer engraving. At the top of the stairs to the second floor is the G.F. Watts *Sea-horses* of which the less said the better.

(ii) The Iveagh Bequest, Kenwood

Hampstead Lane, N.W.3. (See map p.90).
Telephone 01–348–1286.
Opening Hours Every day from 10.00 to 19.00 (April to September), 10.00 to 17.00 (October, February and March), 10.00 to 16.00 or dusk (November, December and January).
Closed Good Friday, Christmas Eve, Christmas Day, New Year's Day.
Admission Free
Parking Space available in the grounds
How to get there Take the 210 Bus from Golders Green or Archway stations, or from Whitestone Ponds, Hampstead.
Facilities Refreshments available in the Coach House and Old Kitchen Restaurant. Postcard and reproduction counters.

In a woodland and lakeside landscaped park setting, Kenwood House is full of eighteenth century elegance at the hands of Robert Adam whose library here was one of his most successful interiors. The decor and the estate would justify a visit on their own, but the main attraction must be a select and famous collection of pictures – one of the nation's finest, and now administered by the GLC.

The Entrance Hall has two large Romney portraits, *Miss Martindale* and *Mrs Musters*, and *Venus Chiding Cupid* by Reynolds, a subject the man the Pre-Raphaelites dubbed 'Sir Sloshua' returned to on two other occasions. Turn left from the Hall and left again into the Marble Hall for eighteenth century French works by Boucher (*Man Offering Grapes to a Girl* and *Landscape with Figures gathering Cherries*) and by Watteau's follower Pater (a pair entitled *Fete Champetre*). The next room, the Dining Room, has two of the greatest works in the collection and indeed in London; Jan Vermeer's *The Guitar Player*, with its cool and exquisite sense of colour and design, subject of a temporary removal by thieves but now happily restored to its rightful place; and one of Rembrandt's finest self-portraits, *Portrait of the Artist*, painted six years before his death, palette in hand and looking at himself in objective yet moving and majestic simplicity. This canvas alone should repay the visit. Also in the room are *Yarmouth Water Frolic* by the Cromes (father and son), Frans Snyders' *Figures with Fruit and Game* (once attributed to Rubens), Albert Cuyp's *View of Dordrecht* (which might be the centre of attraction in less illustrious company), and Frans Hals' *Pieter van de Broecke* ('The Man with a Cane') which has all the virtuosity of his better-known *Laughing Cavalier* in the Wallace Collection (see p. 83) with little of its insufferable conceit.

Pass back through the Marble Hall into the Vestibule, look into the Adam library to the left, and at the pair of Angelica Kauffmans *Rinaldo and Armida* and *Gualtherius and Griselda*, then turn right into the Breakfast Room. The three Reynolds portraits here, *Laughing Girl, Lady Diana Beauclerk* and *Kitty Fisher as Cleopatra dissolving the Pearl*, are of child, aristocrat, and prostitute respectively. Gainsborough's rather poor *Portrait of a Lady*, if it is a Gainsborough, is more than outweighed by his *Going to Market*. The Joseph Wright of Derby, *Dressing the Kitten*, if still present, is on loan to the GLC. The Parlour follows and has Gainsborough's *Pitt*, an excellent early Turner *Fishermen upon a Lee Shore*, *Sea-pieces* by both Van de Veldes, a better *Sea-piece* by Van de Capelle, Romney's *Lady Hamilton at the*

Spinning Wheel (famous but unconvincing) and John Hoppner's *Mrs Jordan as Viola* (another well-known mistress – the sitter had ten illegitimate children by the man who became William IV).

Go through the Old Tea Room and the Boudoir into the Orangery with its view of the grounds and which is dominated by the Stubbs' *Whistlejacket*, a huge equine piece which must surely be the finest painting of a horse ever painted. It needs two Van Dycks to keep it company – *James Stuart, Duke of Richmond* accompanied by a pearl-collared greyhound, and *Henrietta of Lorraine* accompanied by a negro page-boy. A right turn from here takes us into the Lobby for another selection of portraits ranging from flattery laid on as if with a palette knife (Romney's *Lady Hamilton at Prayer*) to the predictable (Reynolds' *Louisa Manners* and *Mrs Muster as Hebe*), and concluding with the ingratiatingly sentimental – a kind of eighteenth century version of Shirley Temple singing the Good Ship Lollipop in Lawrence's *Miss Murray* who proffers her petals like a tray of lollipops.

In the Music Room, Gainsborough reigns in his various guises – the rustic humours of *Two Shepherd Boys with Dogs Fighting*; and the courtly portraiture of *Miss Brummell* (poor) and *Mary, Countess Howe* (full of elegance yet very believable in her pink dress) or *Lady Brisco* (incredibly tall in her silver dress). Two other Reynolds works are here too – *Lady Mary Leslie*, and *Mrs Tollemache as Miranda*.

Return to the Entrance Hall via the Lobby and the narrow corridor (which has two Landseers, *Hawking in the Olden Time* and *The Hon E.S. Russell*).

The Dulwich College Picture Gallery

College Road, S.E.21. (See map p.94).
Telephone 01–693–5254
Opening Hours Tuesday to Saturday 10.00 to 18.00 (May to August), 10.00 to 17.00 (Sept 1st to Oct 15th, and March 16th to April 30th) and 10.00 to 16.00 (Oct 16th to March 15th). Sundays 14.00 to 18.00 (May to August only) and 14.00 to 17.00 (April and September only).
Closed **Mondays** and Good Friday, Christmas Eve, Christmas Day, Boxing Day and New Year's Day.
Admission Free

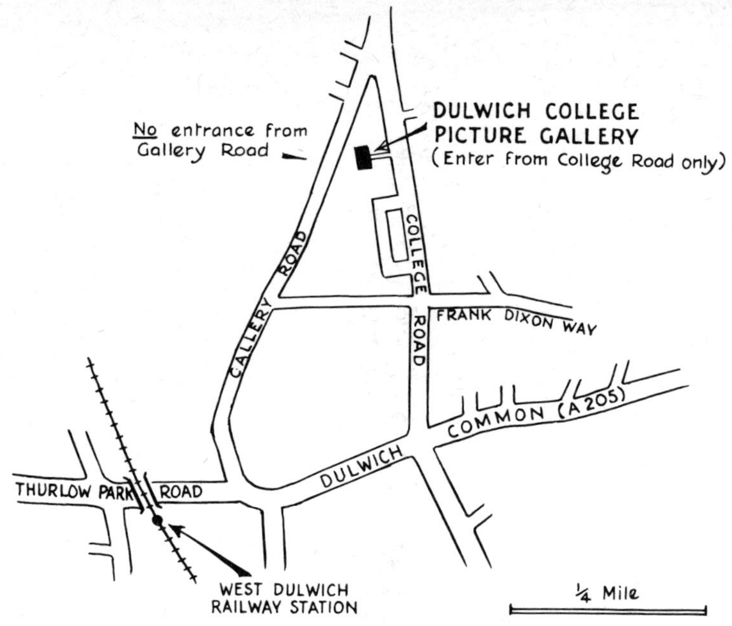

Parking Possible in roads nearby
How to get there **British Rail**: West Dulwich (from Victoria). **Underground**: Brixton then Number 3 bus to Thurlow Park Road. **Buses**: 37, P4 to Dulwich Village; 12, 12a, 78, 176, 176a, 185 to Dulwich Library.
Facilities Postcard counter.

Although the Dulwich gallery has many important works, and no serious art student will exclude it from a list of musts, it has always seemed a little forbidding to me, lacking in some ways the warmth of other lesser collections. Nevertheless, it holds some fine canvasses. On entering the gallery and rounding the central counter where umbrellas should be handed in, and postcards can be purchased, turn left into II and left again into Room XI. This has a small Elsheimer *Susannah and the Elders* in enamel on copper, and three Rembrandts to make you delighted you came. *Girl at the Window* has Rembrandt using a broad technique even for the ruddy cheeks and contrasting strongly with the delicately moulded highlights in *Jacob de Gheyne III*. *Portrait of Titus*,

DULWICH COLLEGE GALLERY

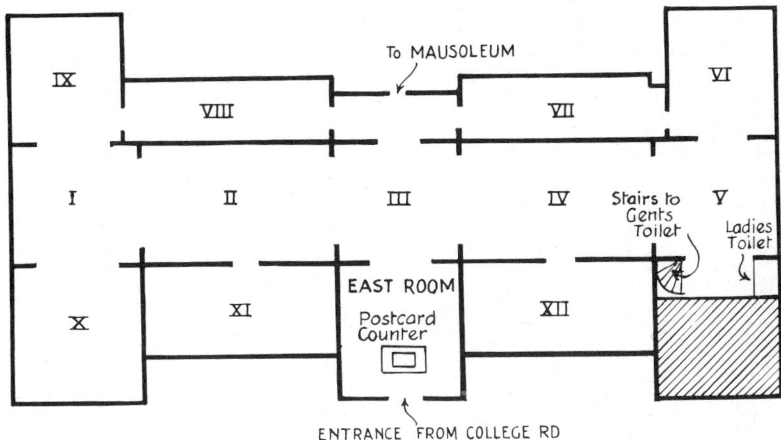

which can usefully be compared with the similar one in the Wallace Collection (see p. 82), has the boy's soft brown eyes looking at his father and us over an embryo adolescent moustache and his red coat lifted from the gloom of the background with heavy slashed brushstrokes. It is a small miracle in paint.

Move back into II for some other Dutch works including Hobbema's *Landscape with Windmill*, a couple of Van Huysum flower pieces, and a group of Cuyps including the large *Cattle near a River*. The end room, Room I, is mainly Italian – Salvator Rosa's *Soldiers Gambling,* Veronese's *Saint and a Venetian Gentleman*, and Guido Reni's *St John the Baptist*, a sort of Caravaggio minus the drama and the sexiness. Room X, just off I, has a Guercino *Woman taken in adultery*, a Lely *Nymphs* and three Murillos – *Two Peasant Boys and a Negro Boy, Two Peasant Boys*, and *The Madonna del Rosario* – which the people who like that sort of thing will find just the sort of thing they like. At the other end of Room I is Room IX with two Canalettos, one good (*Old Walton Bridge*), and one excellent (*The Doge's Palace, Venice*), and a group of Rubens sketches of stunning quality to accompany his *Landscape with Shepherd* and the fine *Venus, Mars and Cupid*. From IX walk through the narrow VIII to see a number of Teniers, a glass case with two tiny Raphael saints on panels, *St Francis* and *St Anthony of Padua*, and Piero di Cosimo's *Portrait of a Young Man*. Continue through VII with more Dutch works, Van de Velde and Ruisdael included, and into VI which is crowded with works including Hogarth's *Portrait of a Gentleman*, Romney's *Haley*, Reynolds' *Infant Samuel* (a pious and sentimental image in which the curly and auburn haired infant raises simultaneously his hand and his eyes heavenward) and *Mrs Siddons as the Tragic Muse* (a dramatic image probably as authentic as Gainsborough's famous portrait in the National Gallery – see p. 12). Here too is a pleasing Richard Wilson landscape, *Tivoli Cascatelli*.

Turn right into V for three large and elegant Gainsborough portraits, *Mrs Moody and her children, The Linley Sisters* (one of whom married Sheridan the playwright and politician), and *Lady and a Gentleman*, and another of his fellow painter *De Loutherbourg*. IV has a small Van Dyck portrait of *William Russell* (which seems to have caught the sitter unawares by the look of his expression and the rumpled hair), an anonymous sixteenth century Flemish *Crucifixion* and Van Dyck's Rubenesque *Samson and Delilah*. Off IV to the left is the unnumbered XII which could well have been transported bodily from the Wallace collection with its rich group of French painters. Watteau's Mozartian *Le Bal Champètre* is the prize canvas in the room and almost of the collection, but Poussin has four works here, two, *Rinaldo and Armida* and *Nurture of Jupiter*, on classical themes, and two, *Triumph of David* and *Flight into Egypt*, on biblical incidents. Lancret's *Fete Champetre*, and Le Brun's *Horatius Codes defending Rome* and *Massacre of the Innocents* are also in this room.

A Trip to Chiswick

Although there are very few pictures to be seen in the vicinity, a visit to Chiswick is a pilgrimage that should be made by anyone interested in one of England's most fascinating painters, William Hogarth. What follows therefore is a brief guide to three places, all within comfortable walking distance of each other, which can be combined in a pleasant morning or afternoon.

(i) Hogarth's House

Hogarth Lane, Chiswick, W.4. (See map p.98).
Telephone 01–994–6757
Opening Hours Monday to Saturday 11.00 to 18.00 (April to September); Monday, Wednesday to Saturday 11.00 to 16.00 (October to March); and Sundays 14.00 to 18.00 (April to September) and 14.00 to 16.00 (October to March).
Closed **Tuesdays October to March,** Good Friday, Christmas Day, Boxing Day and New Year's Day.
Admission Small admission charge.
Parking In road nearby, or car park at public tennis courts fifty yards along A4 just beyond northern gates of Chiswick House Grounds.
How to get there **Underground**: Hammersmith then bus 290.

Set in the high wall which protects the quaint house and garden (with its mulberry tree believed to have been planted by Hogarth himself) from the incessant traffic of the A4 is a door. Ring the bell for admittance. There are no paintings in this house which the great man used as a retreat from his town house (which was on the site of the present Leicester Square) but there is a comprehensive collection of prints which can be studied at leisure. All the likely subjects, satirical, historic and literary are here, though Hogarth was neither a great engraver or etcher and sometimes did not bother to reverse the image in copying the original paintings. However, a visit is strongly recommended to anyone with an interest in Hogarth. It is perhaps instructive also to remember that these prints, the eighteenth century equivalents of today's colour reproductions, were what brought Hogarth his main income.

(ii) St Nicolas Parish Church, Chiswick

On leaving Hogarth's House turn right and walk back to the Hogarth roundabout where the A4 and the A316 meet (see map p.98). On the southern side of the roundabout (use the underground subways to get there) is the George and Devonshire public house (and also to the right of it Boston House, believed to feature in Thackeray's *Vanity Fair*). Running south from the other side of the George and Devonshire is the narrow and charming Church Street which takes one directly to the church. In the churchyard is the urn-topped tomb of Hogarth and also a mausoleum for De Loutherbourg (and in the new burial ground further to the west, by the northern wall is buried James McNeill Whistler).

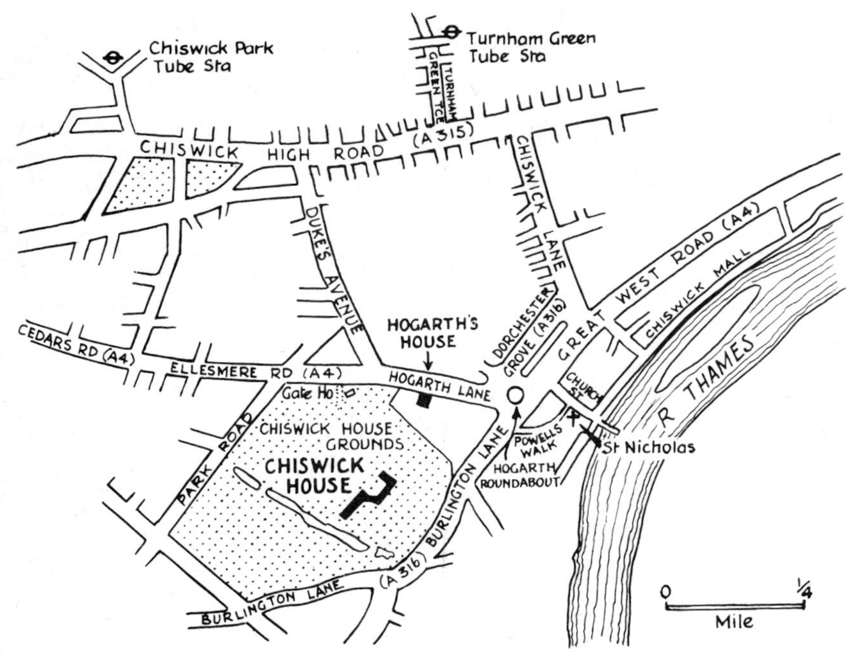

(iii) Chiswick House

Burlington Lane, Chiswick W.4. (See map above)
Telephone 01–994–3299
Opening Hours Every day 09.30 to 13.00 and 14.00 to 17.30 (April); every day 09.30 to 13.00 and 14.00 to 19.00 (May to September); Wednesday to Sunday 09.30 to 13.00 and 14.00 to 17.30 (March and October); Wednesday to Sunday 09.30 to 13.00 and 14.00 to 16.00 (November to February).
Closed **Mondays and Tuesdays from October to March**, Christmas Day, Boxing Day and New Year's Day.
Admission Small admission charge.
Parking Parking in roads nearby.

How to get there **British Rail:** Chiswick (from Waterloo). **Underground:** Hammersmith then bus 290 or long walk from Turnham Green. **Buses:** 290 or E.3.

Chiswick House can also be reached from St Nicolas' Church by taking the lane (Powell's Walk) alongside the Churchyard and turning left at the end into Burlington Lane – the entrance is on the right hand side of Burlington Lane about 100 yards along. Alternatively, on coming out of Hogarth's House turn left and walk along Hogarth Lane (A4) until you come to the northern gates of the grounds on the left hand side, after about 50 yards.

The Palladian villa itself is set within the 60 acres of wooded park which is one of its main attractions. Within the house, the most important room is the Domed Saloon which features eight large pictures; *Charles I and his family* (a copy of a Van Dyck), *The Moroccan Ambassador* by Kneller, two portraits by Ferdinand Elle (*Louis XIII* and *Anne of Austria*), *Liberality and Modesty* by Guido Reni, *Rape of Proserpine* by Anthonie Schoonjans, and two pictures, probably by Daniclo da Volterra, *Apollo and Daphne* and *Judgment of Paris*. The Red Velvet Room has two Sebastiano Riccis – *Diana and Endymion* (left) and *Venus and Cupid* and a William Kent ceiling, while the Blue Velvet Room has *Inigo Jones* by Dobson and *Alexander Pope* by Kent in round panels above the doors. The Gallery has ceiling panels also by Kent, with one central panel either by Veronese, or, more likely, a Ricci copy of the Veronese style. Ricci is also responsible for the overmantel pictures in the Green Velvet Room.

William Morris Gallery and Brangwyn Gift

The Water House, Lloyd Park, Forest Road, Walthamstow, E.17. (See map p.100).
Telephone 01–527–544 Ext. 390.
Opening Hours Monday to Saturday 10.00 to 17.00 (extended to 20.00 on Tuesdays and Thursdays during April to September only). Sundays 10.00 to 12.00 and 14.00 to 17.00 **But only for the first Sunday in each month.**
Closed All other Sundays, Christmas Day, Boxing Day, New Year's Day, Good Friday and all other Bank Holidays.
Admission Free.

Parking In front of house.
How to get there **British Rail**: Walthamstow Central (from Liverpool St) then bus 34, 55 or W21. **Underground**: Walthamstow Central then bus 34, 55 or W21, or Blackhorse Road and a bus 123 along Forest Road. **Greenline Bus**: 718, (Bus Stop, Bell Corner, Walthamstow).

Admirers of the multi-talented Victorian poet, designer, craftsman, typographer, illuminator and socialist, William Morris, will

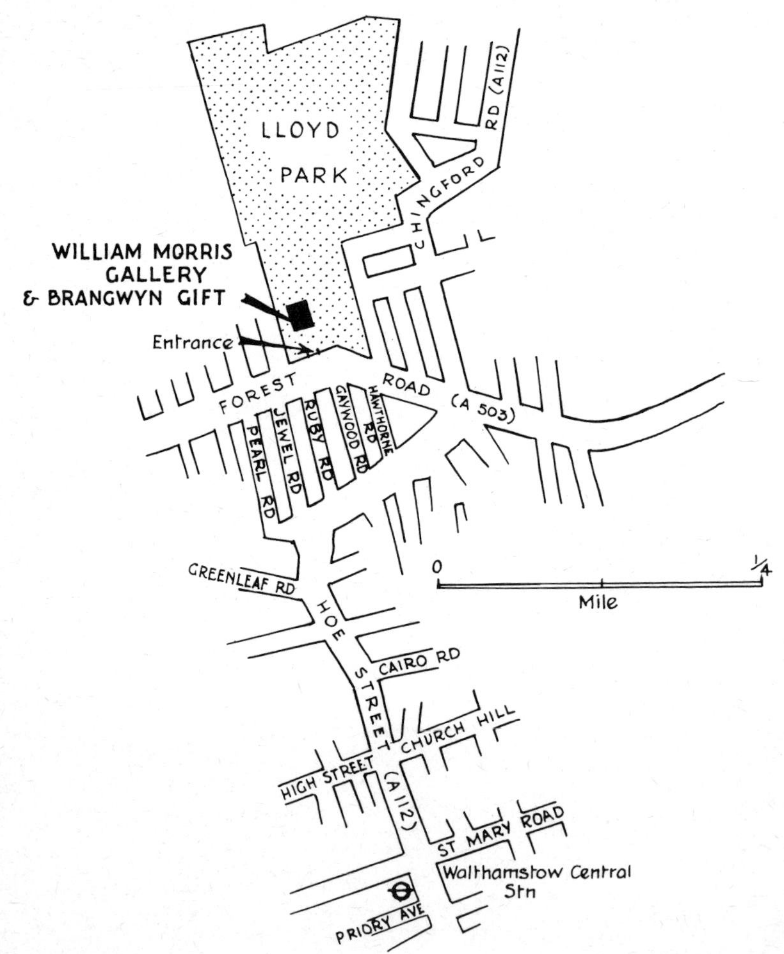

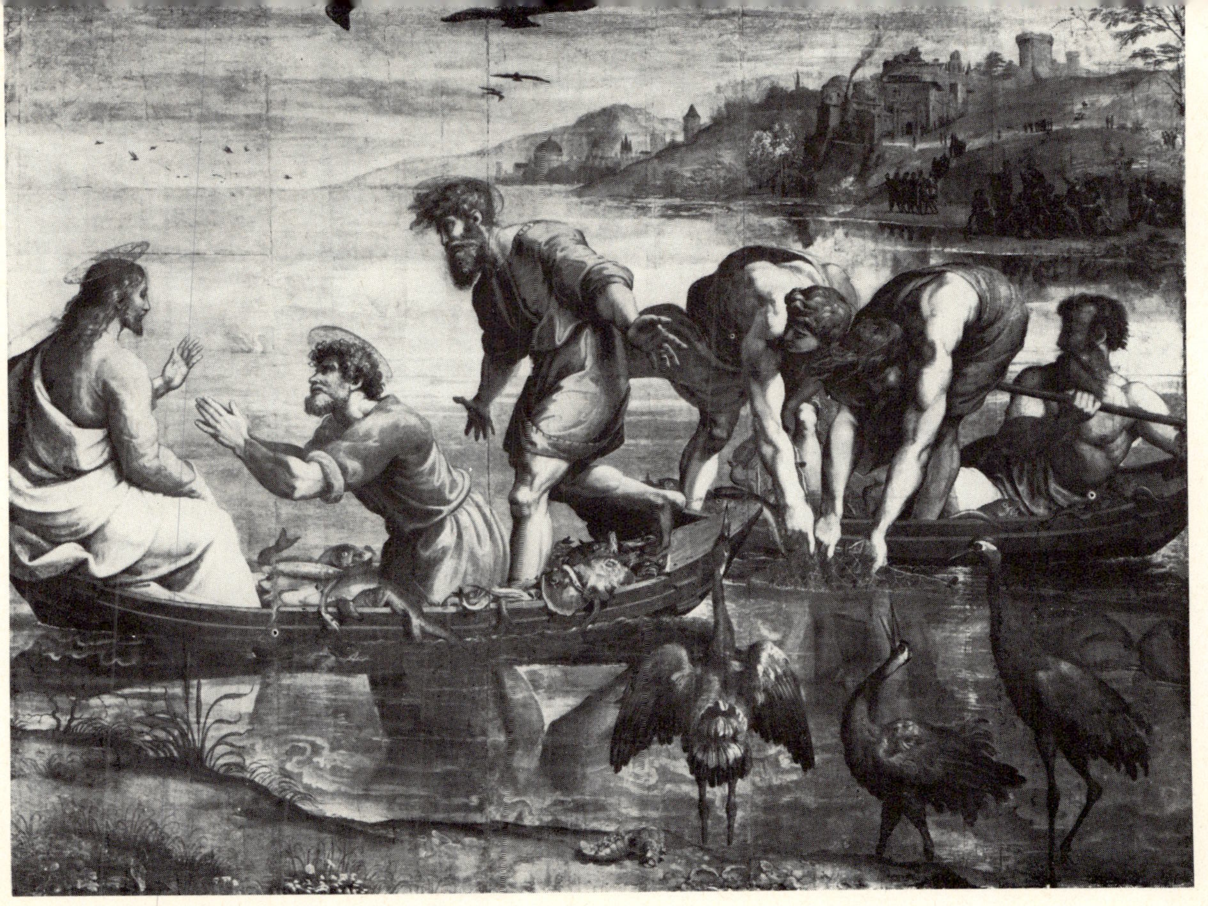

The Miraculous Draught of Fishes by Raphael, *Victoria and Albert Museum*

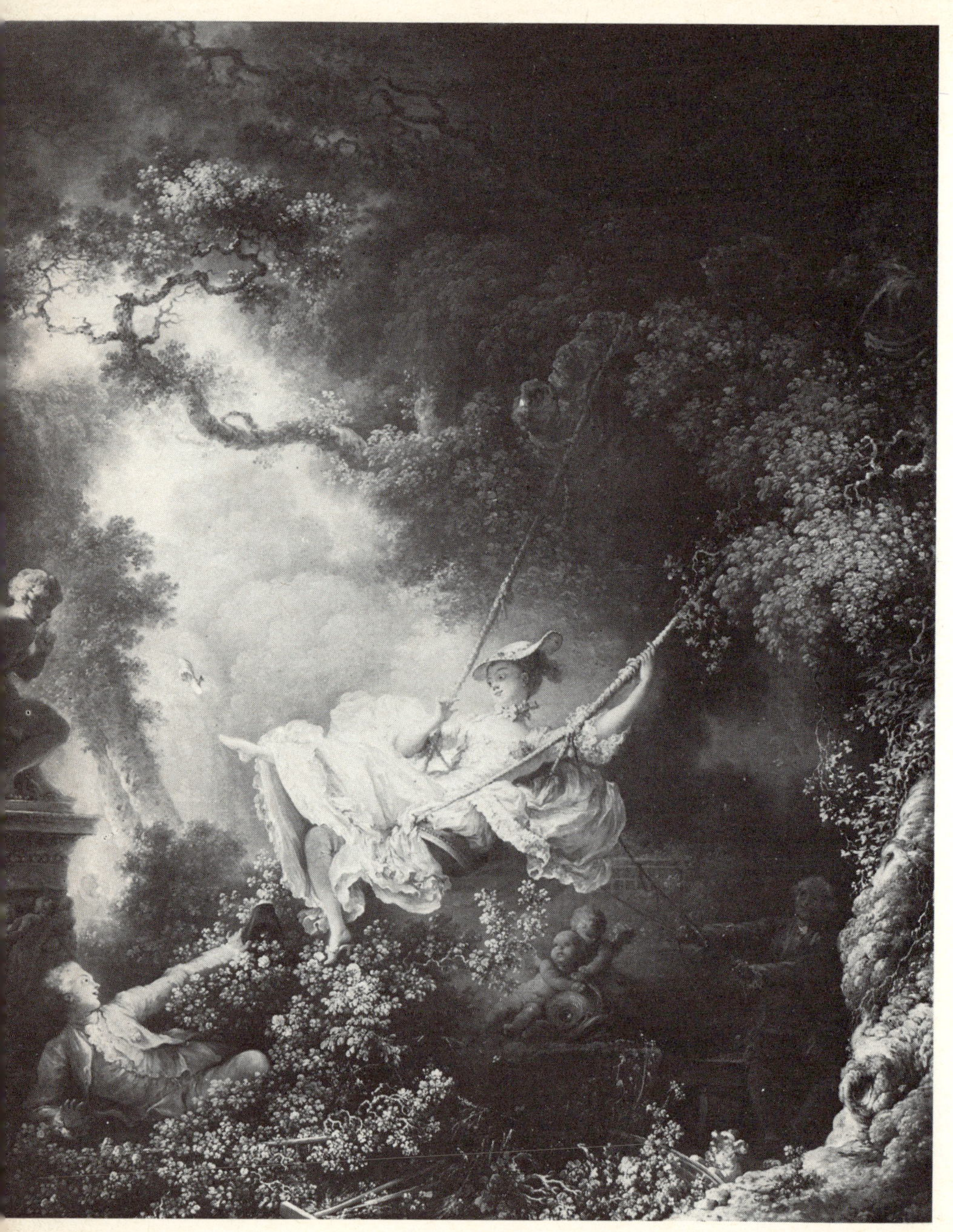

The Swing by Fragonard, *The Wallace Collection*

undoubtedly want to pay a visit to this charming house set in the south part of Lloyd Park. It contains furniture, wallpaper, textiles and (in the library open by appointment only) much documentary material relating to Morris and his circle (who were, of course responsible for the second wave of Pre-Raphaelitism). It is included here because it was the recipient of a number of nineteenth and twentieth century paintings and drawings in Sir Frank Brangwyn's collection. The paintings hung in the house are changed around every few months but include Walter Crane's *Love's Altar* and the dreadful *Angel of Peace*, William Holman Hunt's *Tower of David at Jerusalem* – watercolour, W. Bell Scott's *Seashore*, F.J. Shields' *Angel with the Grail* in red chalk, a Charles Conder, some Alma-Tademas, Arthur Hughes' *He is Risen,* some Rossettis, some Ford Madox Browns, some Burne-Joneses, and a good cross-section of Brangwyn's own work including the *West Indian Market* study, *Venetian Sails*, and a marquetry picture *Hollyhocks* made to his design.

A Trip to Greenwich (i) The Royal Naval College

King William Walk, S.E.10. (See map p.102).
Telephone 01–858–2154.
Opening Hours Monday to Wednesday and Friday to Sunday 14.30 to 17.00.
Closed **Thursdays**, Good Friday, Christmas Eve, Christmas Day.
Admission Free.
Parking Limited parking for visitors near the Cutty Sark nearby.
How to get there **British Rail:** Greenwich or Maze Hill (from Waterloo). **Buses:** 53, 54, 75, 177, 180, 180a, 185. **Boat:** to Greenwich Pier.
Facilities Postcard counter and 'sound-guides' for hire.

Sir Christopher Wren's Royal Naval College is an architectural masterpiece which has two further outstanding features to attract visitors – the Painted Hall and the Chapel. Enter from the gates in King William Walk and walk along the central walk until you come to the steps on the right leading to the Painted Hall. Painted by Sir James Thornhill over nineteen years from 1708 to 1727, the Hall is still used as a dining room for naval officers who are daily privileged to eat surrounded by perhaps the finest expression of the spirit of the baroque in all England. The scope of the design is

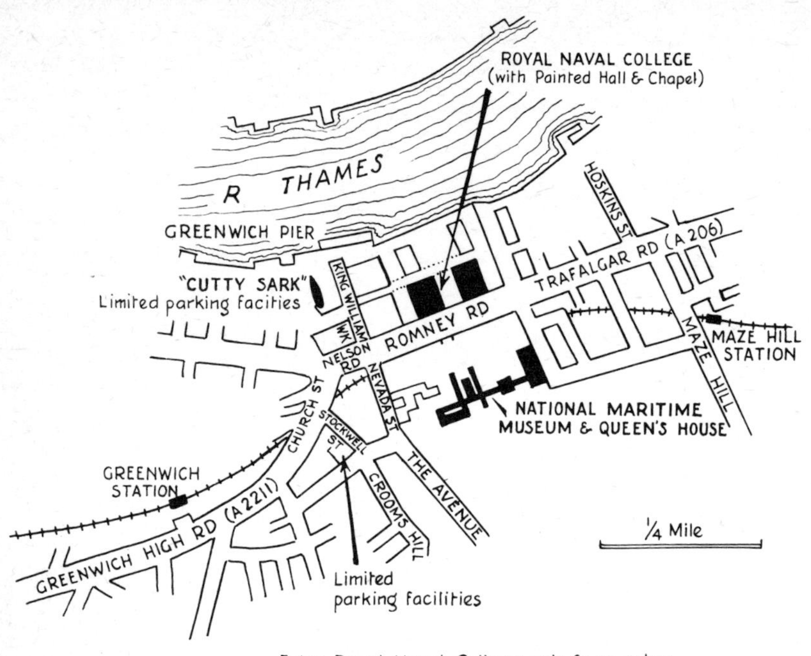

highly dramatic, a swirling teeming composition that spills over from its bounds, celebrating British might based on naval power and the Protestant Succession. When you have regained your breath from your first sight of this magnificent scene, you can begin to decipher the symbols and allegories Thornhill brings to this celebration.

In the central oval, Apollo shines down on William III who receives an olive branch from Peace, hands a red cap of Liberty to Europe (on the white horse) and stamps on Catholic Tyranny (Louis XIV – who else?). Below, Architecture points to a drawing of the original building, and, at the darkened base of the oval, Minerva and Hercules club an assorted group of Vices, the darkness contrasting with the shining light of the heavens. The twelve lunar symbols of the Zodiac are around the oval, and Air, Water, Earth, and Fire are in the corners outside it. The sections at either end with arches show English ships loaded with the Fruits of War; the far end (next to the Upper Hall) shows London, the Thames, the Isis and the Tyne (carrying a sack of coal). The other end (near the entrance) has the Severn (a man with reeds in his hair), the Avon and the Humber, and a number of astronomers – Tycho Brahe, Copernicus, and Flamsteed – the last-named predicts on his piece of paper the April 1715 eclipse of the sun.

On the upper level through the proscenium arch (with its Orange coat of arms) is the West Wall showing the Hanoverian succession inaugurating a new Golden Age of Prosperity. George I and his family are flanked by Victory (right with a scroll of English naval successes). The artist Thornhill himself stands just below her, behind the base of the pillars and perhaps dissatisfied with his fees (at £1 a square yard for the walls, and £3 a square yard for ceilings, he got less than £7,000 for his 19 years work, and had to make a fuss to get that). The upper level ceiling shows the Virtues saluting Queen Anne and George I. Still on the upper level, the right-hand wall shows George I landing at Greenwich and St George slaying the dragon (i.e. Catholicism). The left-hand wall has William landing at Torbay. Both side walls are painted in grisaille, a monochrome technique, to enhance the glorious colouring of the other areas.

On leaving the Painted Hall, cross over to the Chapel – behind the altar is Benjamin West's outsize *Preservation of St Paul after Shipwreck at Malta.*

(ii) The National Maritime Museum

Romney Road, S.E.10 (See map p. 102)
Telephone 01–858–4422.
Opening Hours Monday to Friday 10.00 to 18.00 (Summer) and 10.00 to 17.00 (Winter). Saturday (all the year) 10.00 to 18.00. Sunday (all the year) 14.30 to 18.00
Closed Good Friday, Christmas Eve, Christmas Day, Boxing Day, New Year's Day.
Admission Free.
How to get there **British Rail**: Greenwich or Maze Hill. **Buses**: 70, 177, 180, 185, 228 all pass the museum.
Parking Car parking facilities.

Facilities Bookstalls, postcards and souvenir counters. Restaurant catering temporarily suspended during rebuilding. Reference library available.

The National Maritime Museum has a natural advantage in that it is housed in one of the finest series of buildings in London, for its West Wing and its East Wing and the central Queen's House (built by Inigo Jones as the first Palladian villa in England) are all linked by covered colonnades to form a complex of supreme elegance. It is also a museum which has adopted modern and coherent methods of display and taken elaborate care to make a visitor both welcome and informed. It houses exhibits illustrating the maritime history of Britain in its broadest sense ranging from objects the size of a ship's biscuit, to a full-sized working tug-boat, and includes a vast collection of paintings and drawings of the highest possible quality (1450 prints by the Van de Veldes, for example!).

The West Wing of the museum is undergoing a three year period of reorganisation continuing until 1976 so it is impossible to predict the room-by-room arrangement. However, the general plan of the Museum is to integrate its holdings chronologically. Broadly speaking, this means that the Queen's House covers up to the seventeenth century, the West Wing from 1700–1815, and the East Wing 1815 to date though all the dates are very approximate. Within this framework, will be displayed its major paintings. These include the following: a large number of Van de Veldes, both father and son, most if not all the minor Dutch painters of seventeenth century seascapes, Michael Dahl, Kneller and Lely portraits of naval personalities, Reynolds' *Admiral Lord Keppel*, Canaletto's *Greenwich*, Hogarth's *Captain Sir Alexander Schomberg* and *Captain Lord George Graham in his Cabin* (in which the dog is Hogarth's beloved Trump), De Loutherbourg's *Battle of the Glorious First of June*, early naval scenes by Adam Willarts, and *The Battle of Trafalgar* by Turner.

Syon House ✓

Syon Park, Brentford.
Telephone 01–560–3225
Opening Hours The opening hours are complicated and subject to change, but during 1974 the house was open from the Thursday

before Good Friday until July 26 on Monday, Tuesday, Wednesday, Thursday and Friday and over the Easter weekend. From Sunday July 28th until Sunday September 29th it was open Sunday, Monday, Tuesday, Wednesday and Thursday only. Hours every day are 13.00 to 17.00 *but the last admission tickets are sold at 16.15.*

Closed At all other times.

Admission Charge.

Parking Free car park.

How to get there **British Rail:** Syon Lane (from Waterloo); **Underground:** Hammersmith and bus 267; Gunnersbury and buses 117 or 267. **Buses:** E1, E2, 37, 117, 267. **Greenline Bus:** 701 (to Isleworth Gate).

Facilities Cafeteria, bars and restaurant in the grounds which also hold a gardening centre, gardens, an aquarium and a London Transport historical collection.

This, the summer home of the Duke of Northumberland, full of sumptuous Adam interiors, is set in riverside parkland landscaped by Capability Brown. The Great Hall with black and white marble tiles and Doric columns sets a classical tone, and the grandiose Ante Room with a brilliant scagliola floor is pure Roman Empire (scagliola is an imitation stone made of plaster and glue which lends itself to vivid colouring and a highly polished finish). In the Dining Room, the chiaroscuro frieze panels are by Andrea Casali who came to England from Italy in 1748. The Red Drawing Room hung with plum-coloured Spitalfields silk has a ceiling decorated by Giovanni Battista Cipriani (a founder of the Royal Academy, he designed the RA Diploma and also the panels of the Coronation Coach). It also has a number of Peter Lely portraits – *Charles I, James Duke of York, Princess Elizabeth* (Charles I's daughter), *Charles I and the Duke of York* – as well as the *Queen Henrietta Maria* by Van Dyck.

The Long Gallery which looks over the Thames to Kew Gardens has two landscapes by Francesco Zuccarelli over the chimney-pieces, and the Print Room, among other portraits, has *The First Duke of Northumberland* by Gainsborough and *The First Duchess* by Reynolds. In the Oak Passage, look for *Belshazzar's Feast* painted on glass by the spectacular John Martin.

Ham House ✓

Petersham Road, Nr Richmond, Surrey (See map p.107).
Telephone 01–940–1950
Opening Hours Tuesday to Sunday 14.00 to 18.00 (April to September) also Bank Holiday Mondays; and Tuesday to Sunday 12.00 to 16.00 (October to March).
Closed **Mondays** other than Bank Holidays, Good Friday, Christmas Eve, Christmas Day, Boxing Day, and New Year's Day.
Admission Charge.
Parking Car park only from Ham Street entrance.
How to get there **British Rail/Underground:** Richmond then 71 (Mon to Sat), 65 or 65a bus to Fox and Duck Inn, Petersham. **Greenline Bus:** 714, 716, 716a (from Hyde Park Corner) to Dysart Arms, Petersham.
Facilities Restaurant and tea garden at side of house open from 14.30 to closing time April to September only.

A modest country residence when built in 1610, Ham House was extended after the Restoration to become as sumptuous an example of its late seventeenth century period as any. It may not have today all the trappings of that luxurious age, but more than enough of its character and magnificent furnishings remain to make for a superb afternoon's viewing.

The house is full of pictures distributed throughout its 24 rooms, many of them copies and many relatively undistinguished. There are however some which call for special attention. In the Great Hall, the portraits include *Henrietta Cavendish* by Kneller, *Lyonel Tollemache* by John Vanderbank, and *Charlotte Walpole* by Reynolds. The mis-named Marble Dining Room has rare gilt-leather hangings and a parquetry floor, and among other works there is the odd *Fantastic Landscape* over the middle door by a follower of Bosch. The Duke's Dressing Room has *Wooded Landscape with Dogs* by A. Bega in the centre opposite the windows, *Classical Ruins with Christ and the Woman of Canaan* by Bartholomeus Breenbergh to the left of it, and an imitation Bassano of *Orpheus charming the animals* to the right. In the Duchess' Bedchamber, the two paintings over the doors, and the two upright pictures either side of the alcove, are all *Sea-Pieces* by

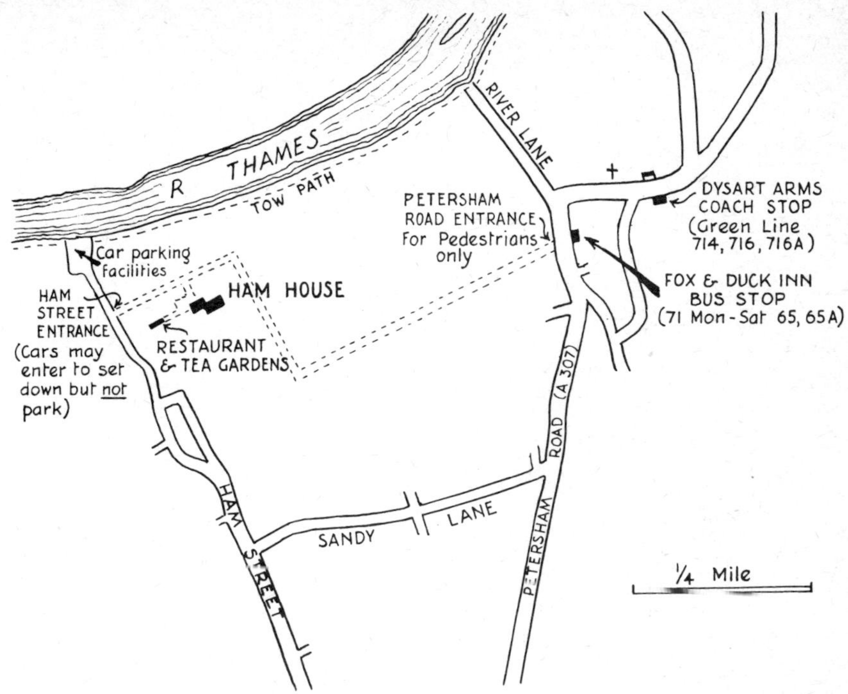

Van de Velde the Younger. *The Duke of Lauderdale* is a crayon study by Edmund Ashfield over the fireplace and opposite it is *Elizabeth Dysart with her first husband Lyonel Tollemache and her sister Lady Maynard* attributed to Joan Carlile and one of the very first 'conversation pieces' ever painted in England. The small Duke's Closet has Thomas Wyck's *Alchemist* and another Van de Velde *Sea-Piece*.

In the Yellow Bedchamber with flamboyant plum-coloured bed drapings, the tapestries are taken from Poussin paintings in the Louvre, and the two bird paintings are by Francis Barlow. The White Closet, with a Verrio ceiling, includes *Salome and Virgin and Child* by Jacques Stellaert, a friend of Poussin's. The Great Staircase leading to the first floor is hung with poor copies of Titian and Correggio but the landing has the lively *Battle of Lepanto* probably by Cornelius Vroom.

To the left of the stairs, Lady Maynard's Chamber has Vanderbank's *Grace Carteret*, two early commissioned paintings

HAM HOUSE

WHITE CLOSET 8
YELLOW BEDCHAMBER 7
WITHDRAWING ROOM 6
MARBLE DINING ROOM 2
DUKE'S DRESSING ROOM 3
DUCHESS'S BEDCHAMBER 4
DUKE'S CLOSET 5
INNER HALL 10
GREAT HALL 1
Up
CHAPEL 9
ENTRANCE
GROUND FLOOR
LADY MAYNARD'S DRESSING ROOM 13
LADY MAYNARD'S CHAMBER 12
QUEEN'S CLOSET 24
QUEEN'S BEDCHAMBER 23
ANTECHAMBER TO THE QUEEN'S BEDCHAMBER 22
LIBRARY CLOSET 20
14 BEDCHAMBER WITHIN
LIBRARY 21
Down
ROUND GALLERY 16
NORTH DRAWING ROOM 17
LONG GALLERY 19
GREEN CLOSET 18
MUSEUM ROOM 15
FIRST FLOOR

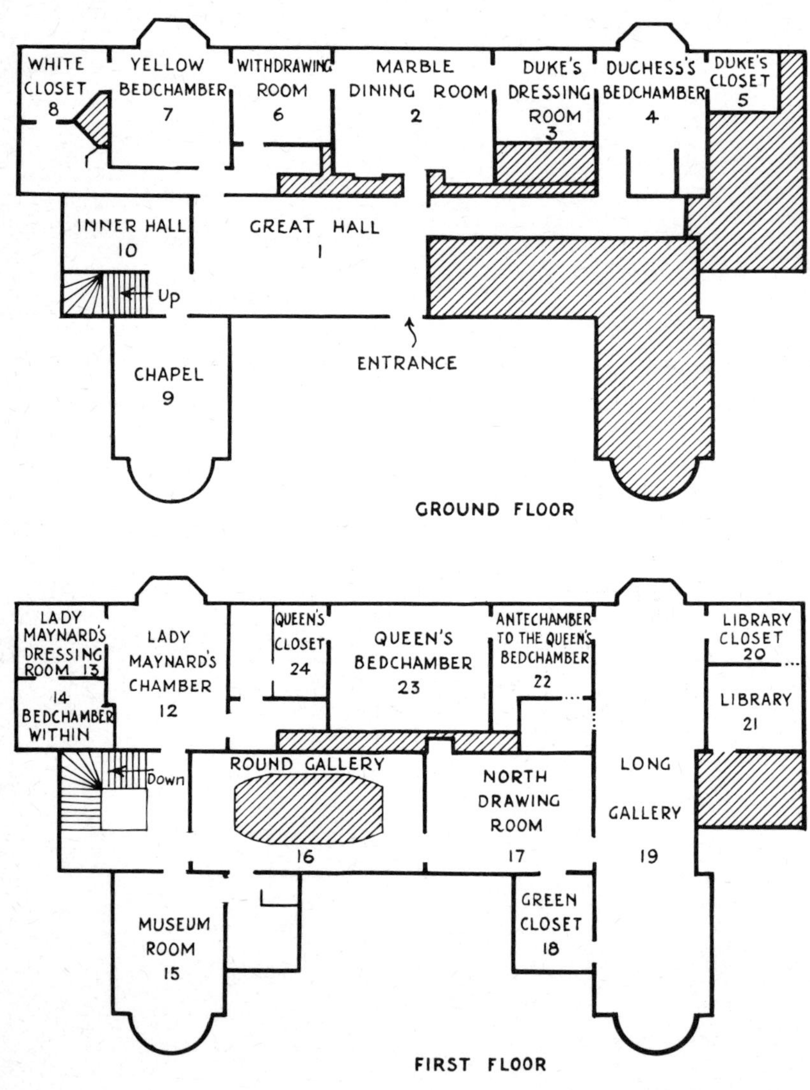

by John Constable – copies of Reynolds and Hoppner – and two, *Thomas Tollemache* and *Frances Worsley*, by Kneller. Lady Maynard's Dressing Room has a case of drawings in Indian ink on vellum by David Paton, and a case of miniatures including some by Nicholas Hilliard, Isaac Oliver, and Samuel Cooper – the masters of the *genre*. To the right of the stairs is the Round Gallery. This has Cornelius Johnson's notable *Dukes of Hamilton and Lauderdale* and his *Unknown Young Man*, the almost monochrome *Daniel in the Lions' Den* is perhaps by Bassano. Here also is a superb portrait of the young *Elizabeth Dysart* by Lely. For full effect, this tender and romantic view with the waterfall in the background should be compared with the work a few yards away of *The Duke and Duchess of Lauderdale* also by Lely more than twenty years later. Here the arch and knowing lady is what the pretty and innocent young girl has become – a sobering thought and not much of an advertisement for marriage to the rough, scheming Lauderdale (he represented the 'L' in the famous or infamous 'CABAL' – the secret 1673 faction under Charles II and the precursor of modern cabinets), or for that matter for Oliver Cromwell, whose mistress she was at one time rumoured to be.

On passing through the North Drawing Room, glance at the fireplace. Is there something familiar about the twisted pillars to left and right? Yes, they were copied from the Raphael cartoon of *The Healing of the Lame Man,* now in the V and A (see p. 54), by the German designer Francis Cleyn. And another piece of his 'borrowings' can be seen in the Green Closet next door, where his tempera-on-paper ceiling has figures remarkably like some Polidoro Caldara paintings at Hampton Court.

The Long Gallery has a number of Lely's portraits, predictably, for he was tremendously fashionable during the reign of Charles II. *Elizabeth, Countess of Dysart with a Black Servant* and *Lady Maynard* are two particularly fine examples among them, but note also *William Murray, Earl of Dysart* by Cornelius Johnson and the excellent *Colonel John Russell* by John Michael Wright. Pass through the Antechamber to the Queen's Bedchamber, which is a positive riot of Oriental lacquer, to the Queen's Bedchamber itself where the tapestries are taken from Watteau and Pater, and where the two paintings over the doors, *Landscape* and *Pair of Lions with a Leopard in a Den*, are by Dirck van den Bergen. The

Queen's Closet next door, with more Thomas Wyck pictures, leads back to the head of the stairs.

Osterley Park House ✓

Jersey Road, Hounslow, Middlesex (See map p.111).
Telephone 01–560–3918.
Opening Hours Tuesday to Sunday 14.00 to 18.00 (April to September) also Bank Holiday Mondays; and Tuesday to Sunday 12.00 to 16.00 (October to March).
Closed **Mondays** other than Bank Holidays, Good Friday, Christmas Eve, Christmas Day, Boxing Day and New Year's Day.
Admission Charge.
Parking Car park in grounds.
How to get there **Underground**: Osterley. **Buses**: 91, 116. **Greenline Buses**: 704, 705.
Facilities Tea rooms near house in old stables with some of the original stalls still showing.

Originally built for the Elizabethan merchant Sir Thomas Gresham in the 1570's, Osterley was completely revamped by the indefatigable Robert Adam about two centuries later, and it remains a fine example of Adam decoration looking as fresh and colourful as if it had been painted yesterday. Most of his specially designed furniture is also intact.

The house holds less paintings than Ham House, but the choice is more select. Turn right on entering the pale icy-blue and white Hall with its black and white marble floor into the North Passage and walk along to the Breakfast Room at the end. Here, if you can take it, is a bright yellow colour scheme with marine blue-green decorations. The rope placed to save the eighteenth century Persian carpet does not make it easy to see all of the paintings but they include van Veerendael's pleasant *Flower Piece*, Julius Caesar Ibbetson's *Landscape with Rustic Bridge and Stream*, Richard Wilson's *Landscape with Venus and Adonis*, *Captain Read* by Angelica Kauffmann, an imitation Bronzino *Lady in a Black Slashed Dress* and an Allan Ramsay (probably) *Young Man.*

The Library features eleven frieze insets by Antonio Zucchi on classical themes (he married Angelica Kauffman, who was often commissioned by Robert Adam). The North Passage, alongside the

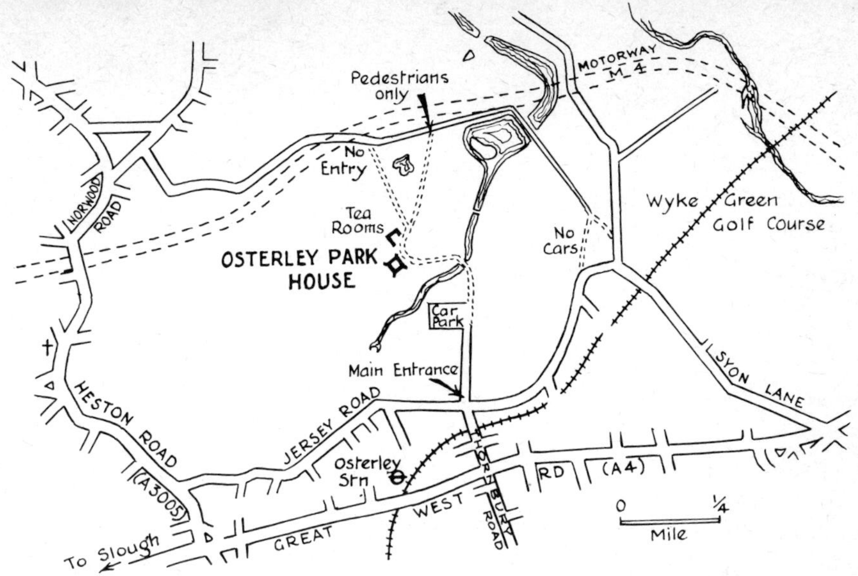

Library, has a number of Adam's drawings and designs behind the blue curtains protecting them from the light, and leads on to the inelegantly-named Eating Room, all green and pink, and featuring more Zucchi insets. They represent (above the doors) *Europe, Asia, Africa,* and *America* and (large at either end) *Moorish Dancers in Turkish Dresses* and *Ruins of A Turkish Bath*, and (over the fireplace) *An Offering to Ceres*. The other doorway from here leads into the Gallery which commands a pleasing view of the grounds. The large portraits on the end walls are *Frederica Charlotta*, daughter of Frederick William II of Prussia, and at the far end her husband *Frederick, Duke of York* (George III's second son). Both are by Hoppner. The Beauvais tapestries dating from the 1780's include a celebration of the then recent American War of Independence. Moving on to the Drawing Room, we see a group of Reynolds' portraits – *Jane, Countess of Eglinton* (large with the sitter playing a harp), *Thomas Middleton Trollope* and *Isabella Thorold* (both small), and *Mrs Powys and her daughter* (large). The painting gracing the fireplace is Richard Wilson's *Landscape with Temple of Clitumnus near Spoleto*. (Wilson was profoundly influenced by the work of Claude and spent four years in Italy painting Italian landscapes.)

The tour ends with the State Bedroom, the Etruscan Room

OSTERLEY PARK HOUSE

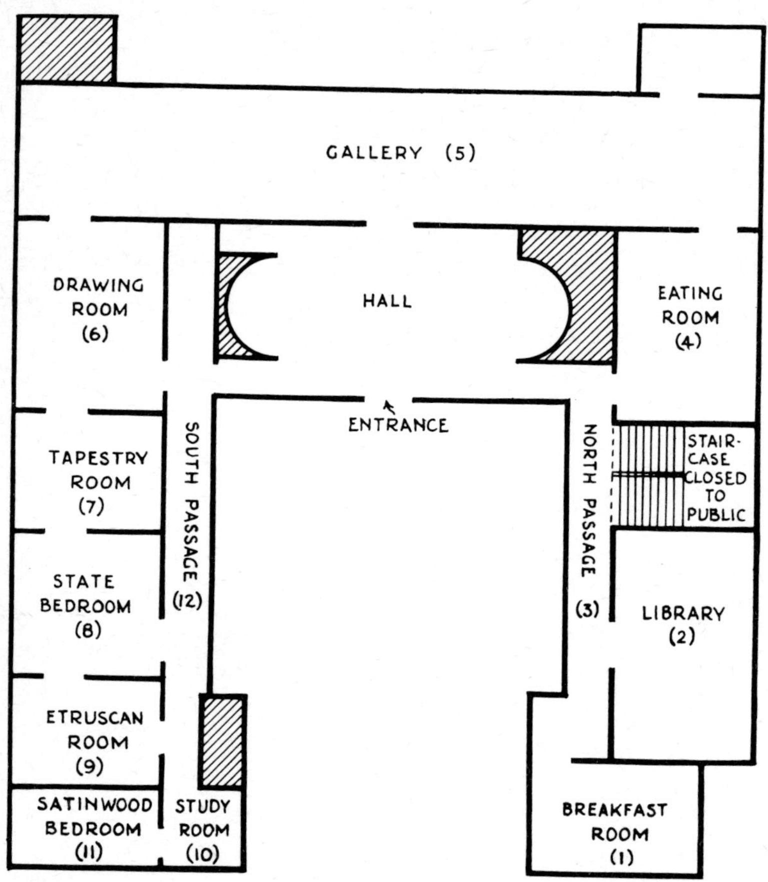

NOTE:- The rooms at Osterley Park House are not numbered
The figures on the plan only represent a suggested viewing order

(decorated by P.M. Borgnis), the Study (with some Adam drawings), and the Satinwood Bedroom. From the Study, the South Passage takes us back to the Hall. On our way through the Passage we pass first a Romney portrait of *Mrs Maxwell* (in woodland setting) and then a Raeburn portrait of *Mrs Stewart of Physgill*.

The Royal Holloway College

Egham Hill, Egham, Surrey.
Telephone Egham 4455
How to get to the College It is necessary to make special arrangements (see text below)*. The College is situated on the left-hand side of the A30 on the way to Virginia Water from Egham (look for the pedestrian bridge over the road) and has its own car park. By public transport there are two alternatives. 1. Take the train to Egham (from Waterloo) and either walk up Egham Hill (25 mins at least) or take a local bus to the College. 2. Take a Greenline bus from London 701, 718, or 725 – all stop outside the College.

*Housed in one of the most imposing Victorian buildings in England, the College is by no means a conventional art gallery, and *it is impossible to gain admittance to its Picture Gallery without prior arrangement*. This is because the Gallery also houses College music rehearsals, and similar events. However, the College gives sympathetic consideration to students and visitors who wish to see their pictures, and providing reasonable notice can be given on both sides, will arrange a mutually satisfactory time for viewing. Contact the Secretary's Department, preferably by post, giving an address or telephone number where you can be contacted.

Once you have successfully negotiated the preliminaries, the collection offers one of the best cross-sections of English Victorian painting to be seen anywhere. The brilliant, the banal, the historic, the narrative, the literary, the sentimental and the masterpiece are all represented here. On entering the main doors of the Room look above the lintel for Clarkson Stanfield's *Battle of Roveredo* (a battle actually fought between France and Austria in the Tyrol in 1796 and the pictorial excuse here for a picturesque Alpine setting). The artist, who was a friend of Charles Dickens, was at one time a scene-painter at the Drury Lane theatre. The left hand wall has George Morland's *The Carrier preparing to set out*, J.C. Horsley's *The Banker's Private Room, Snowscape 8* by L. Munthe (an imaginatively lit Norwegian winter sunset by a Norwegian artist), and Clarkson Stanfield's *Pic du Midi, D'Ossau* (very high on the wall but an adroitly handled and splendidly coloured mountain landscape with cloud-capped snowy peaks, yet managing to avoid all the clichés). Next is Landseer's *Man Proposes, God Disposes* worth concentrated study. In a desolated Polar waste, two polar bears painted in free creamy-white brushstrokes rend fragments of a Union Jack and crunch on the remnants of a human rib-cage. Inspired by the finding of the relics of an explorer Sir John Franklin, this was a deliberately sensational picture, but the more one looks at the consummate skill with which the animals are painted, and the grey-green rocks and floes, lit by two patches of pink light, the angrier one becomes that so talented an artist finished up pandering to the sentimental tastes of his public for coy animals with human characteristics. Sentiment is what has wrecked Briton Rivière's *Sympathy*, with its cute dog and its too cute little girl. John Bagnold Burgess' *Licensing the Beggars, Spain* feeds a different prejudice – the one that all beggars, mendicants, and welfare receivers are by nature deceitful rogues sponging on the rest of us (The 'blind' beggar in the foreground casts an eye on the day's gains). Above the door at the far end of the room is Daniel Maclise's *Peter the Great at Deptford Dockyard*.

The long right-hand wall has John Pettie's *A State Secret*, and W.P. Frith's *The Railway Station*. Like Frith's *Derby Day* in the Tate it is packed with types rather than individuals, and part of the fun is meant to be in deciphering the meaning of the incidents – the detectives to the right apprehending a fugitive are portraits of two well-known Victorian detectives, next to them a bride parts from her bridesmaids, in the foreground a cabman and a foreigner shout at each other in mutual incomprehension. It is the old story of Victorian painting trying desperately to imitate the Victorian novel. (The family slightly left of centre is Frith's and the father a self-portrait.) The wall continues with Gainsborough's *Going to Market*, John Linnell's *The Wayfarers*, Edwin Long's *The Suppliants*, Millais' *The Princes in the Tower* (Millais at his worst), John Crome's *Woodland Scene*, and then, tucked behind a maroon curtain which pulls back to reveal it, the finest picture in the collection, Turner's *Van Tromp going about to please his Masters* with a pale blue sky and a foaming grey sea.

Millais' *Princess Elizabeth in Prison at St James* outdoes his

Princes for clichés, and Edwin Long's *The Marriage Market, Babylon* makes sure that its eleven dusky beauties offer their attractions to us the spectators rather than to the bidding Babylonians in the background – and very titillating they are too. Back in the realms of English landscape, the John Constable here, *View on the Stour*, with its rich dark green foliage and threatening sky, would alone be worth travelling to see – like the Turner it is a picture worthy of its painter.

Hampton Court Palace: State Apartments

Hampton Court, Middlesex
Telephone 01–997–8441
Opening Hours (State Apartments only) Monday to Saturday 09.30 to 18.00 (May to September), 09.30 to 17.00 (October, March and April), 09.30 to 16.00 (November to February). Sunday 11.00 to 18.00 (May to September), 14.00 to 17.00 (October, March and April), 14.00 to 16.00 (November to February). In all cases the last tickets are sold half an hour before closing.
Closed Good Friday, Christmas Eve, Christmas Day, Boxing Day and New Year's Day.
Admission Small charge.
Parking Special car park in grounds.
How to get there **British Rail**: Hampton Court (from Waterloo); **Buses**: 111, 131, 152, 201, 206, 211, 216, 264, 267; **Greenline Buses**: 716, 716a, 718, 725.
Facilities Postcards, slides and souvenir counters. The Palace is set in extensive gardens which are open to visitors and there is a cafeteria and a licensed restaurant. Lecture tours during summer only.

A visit to Hampton Court Palace to see the 500 or so pictures distributed throughout the State Apartments should be an unalloyed pleasure. Two things prevent it being so – in many cases the pictures are hung behind the ropes keeping the public away from the furniture and therefore impossible to see properly; and secondly, some pictures have no identification at all, and some show two conflicting attributions at the same time! Considering the vast numbers of visitors who pour through the rooms every summer, it is not the most helpful of policies to follow.

That said, this large section of the Royal Collection has to be seen, for it has important paintings and also some fascinating painted ceilings and walls. The entrance to the State Apartments is in the corner of the Clock Court. Leading up to the first floor where the rooms are, is the King's Staircase painted by Antonio Verrio in about 1700, very elaborate, very colourful and full of obscure political references. The lower part, alongside the lower flight of the stairs, shows Apollo, with a lyre, at the head of a set of figures including Muses, River Gods and the like. The largest wall shows Romulus (with an odd-looking 'wolf') inviting a row of Roman Emperors to a celestial banquet just as Nemesis (right, in mid air with fiery sword) threatens them, and Hercules (with a club) sits on a cloud left. The landing wall (signed by Verrio in the bottom right hand corner) shows Mercury dictating a letter to Julian the Apostate. The last two are probably based on Julian's *Satire on the Caesars*, but how they translate into terms of the seventeenth century and William III, I do not know.

From the landing, walk through the King's Guard Room (with sales counters for postcards etc) and turn left into the First Presence Chamber (helpfully, all the rooms are marked with their title above the doorways). It has Sir Godfrey Kneller's vast *William III* and his eight excellently painted 'Hampton Court Beauties' painted for Queen Mary II. Lely's *Mary of Modena* is over the fireplace. The Second Presence Chamber has Titian's *Portrait of a Man*, Tintoretto's *Esther and King Ahasuerus*, two Polidoro Caldara panels (copied by Francis Cleyn at Ham House see p. 109), Dosso Dossi's *St William*, Bassano's *Adoration of Shepherds*, and a possible Bellini *A Concert*. The Audience Chamber has a number of Tintorettos – *Portrait, The Nine Muses, A Knight of Malta* and *A Dominican* – a number of works by followers of Titian and Veronese, and an interesting brooding portrait of *Andre Odoni* with antique casts, by Lotto. The King's Drawing Room has two Titians (*Lucretia*, and *The Lovers* where the man takes distinct liberties with his partner's chest appendages), two Bassanos (*Jacob's Journey* and *Self-Portrait*), Correggio's *St Catherine*, Del Sarto's *Madonna and Child* and a very odd Dosso Dossi *Holy Family* where the Child embraces a cockerel. William III's Bedroom features a Verrio ceiling of pale yet garish colours with Morpheus holding a sleeping Endymion in his arms. The other paintings are behind the rope but include an interesting Domenico Feti *David* where the boy hero has a giant sword and sits on Goliath's severed head. Another Verrio ceiling in which Venus cradles Mars, graces the King's Dressing Room and, maddeningly behind the rope, are Mabuse's *Adam and Eve*, Holbein's *Noli Me Tangere* and Ulrich Apt's quaint *Man and his Wife*. In the Writing Closet, Guilio Romano's anaemic *Isabella D'Este* competes with Parmigianino's *Minerva* and *Portrait of a Boy*. Queen Mary's Closet next door has an extremely interesting small group of German and Flemish pictures, mainly of the sixteenth century. Pieter Breughel the Elder's *Massacre of the Innocents* reminds one of a Lowry with its quaint figures outlined against the snow. However, closer inspection reveals that the 'innocents' are not babies as one would expect (and as Breughel painted in a number of other versions of the theme in Cambridge and Brussels for example) but domestic pets and farmyard animals. Has the work been tampered with at a later stage with animals painted over the babies to alleviate what would be graphic horrors, perhaps? The excellent picture next to it could be *The Money Changers* in the manner of van Reymerswaele, or *The Misers* by van de Capelle after Quentin Massys – the frame gives both versions! The former is perhaps more likely. Also in the room are three small works by the rare Pieter Cornelisz, and three by Lucas Cranach, *The Fourteen Helpers, Judgment of Paris* and the excellent *Adam and Eve* where Eve sits side-saddle fashion on a kneeling stag.

Walk through the Queen's Gallery to the Queen's Bedroom, the paintings here are roped off but Thornhill's ceiling shows Aurora rising from the sea. The Queen's Drawing Room next door has Verrio decorations with Queen Anne attended by a lion and some hefty nudes on the ceiling; with Prince George of Denmark in his Lord High Admiral role on the wall over the fireplace; and with Cupid in a sea-shell drawn by seahorses on the left-hand wall. Hidden behind the state bed, is another wall showing Anne heralded by the rest of the world. The Queen's Audience Chamber has other portraits out of view and Paul Jan Somer's *Anne of Denmark* over the fireplace. The large Public Dining Room has a selection of Sebastiano Ricci works (with a *Christ in the House of Simon* very like Veronese) and a few by his nephew Marco Ricci. The Prince of Wales' Presence Chamber holds some brilliant earlier Italian works including Gentile da Fabriano's *Madonna and Child* altarpiece, Duccio's *Triptych,* and Bernardo Daddi's *Marriage of the Virgin.*

The Prince of Wales' Drawing Room has Mantegna's *The Vase Bearers,* the only one of his *Triumph of Caesar* series of tempera paintings presently on display. (The series which is almost the chief glory of the Royal Collection awaits the restoration of the lower Orangery which has been undergoing rebuilding for the last ten years – the opening of the restored room may, however, take place shortly.) The adjoining bedroom leads out to the Prince of Wales' staircase (decorated with tapestries perhaps copied from Van de Velde). On the landing nearby is Tintoretto's dark, mysterious and pagan *The Labyrinth of Love*. The series of oak-panelled rooms following, includes the Queen's Private Chapel with Martin Van Heemskerk's *Death and Judgement*, an anonymous Flemish sixteenth century *Virgin and Child and Saints*, Garofalo's *Holy Family*, and Georges De La Tour's *St Jerome*. Paintings in the other rooms are often difficult to see but note the long Cartoon Gallery which once housed Raphael's cartoons where seventeenth century tapestries copied from them now serve instead. The Communication Gallery holds Lely's brilliant series of portraits of ten of the ladies surrounding Charles II and known as 'The Windsor Beauties' – in the middle of them over the fireplace is Lely's *Charles II* himself. The occasional Giordano appears here too.

In the set of rooms off to the left – the Cumberland Suite – can be seen some sixteenth century panels in the Wolsey Closet, and, in the green velvet room, a Domenichino *St Catherine*, a Van Dyck *Charles, Prince of Wales* and a Sebastiano Ricci *The Continence of Scipio*.

After the Suite, move on to the Queen's State Staircase. This has a magnificent allegorical painting by Gerrit van Honthorst, a Dutch painter who worked for Charles I, who appears in the work as Jupiter. The Haunted Gallery has a door which leads to the Royal Pew overlooking the Chapel Royal – the Pew has a Thornhill ceiling. Thornhill also painted the *trompe l'oeil* window in the Chapel itself. Just outside the Pew are Jan Provost's *Triptych* and an anonymous altarpiece of the sixteenth century. The second half of the Haunted Gallery has a striking portrait of *Cardinal Richelieu* by Philippe de Champaigne. The Gallery leads on to the Horn Room and the Great Hall, two of the Palace's greatest attractions to conclude the tour, but with no pictures to rival their architectural splendours.

Windsor Castle: State Apartments

Castle Hill, Windsor, Berks.
Telephone Windsor 68286
Opening Hours Monday to Saturday 10.30 to 17.00 (March to October); 10.30 to 15.00 (January, February, November, December), Sunday 13.30 to 17.00 (**March to October only**)
Closed **Whenever the Queen is in official residence** i.e. usually for part of March, the whole of April, and for periods during May, June and December. Also **Sundays from November to February.**
Admission A small charge
Parking Car park at foot of Windsor Hill.
How to get there **British Rail:** Windsor and Eton Central (from Paddington), Windsor and Eton Riverside (from Waterloo). **Greenline Buses:** 704, 705, 718, 725.
Facilities Commercial bookshop in Castle courtyard.
(N.B. *Exhibition of Drawings by Holbein, Leonardo and others* Opening hours as for the State Apartments but does not close when the Queen is in residence. Closed Good Friday, Christmas Day, Boxing Day and New Year's Day. Small additional charge).

The major part of the sumptuous Royal collection, not held at the V & A, Buckingham Palace or Hampton Court or buried away from public view at Balmoral or Sandringham, makes its appearance at Windsor. Although further from London than any other gallery in this book, its importance and its relative ease of access from the capital make a visit imperative. The paintings generally are of the highest quality, but it has to be said that they are in some cases at an unsatisfactory distance from the poor spectator who is kept behind the ropes. The attendants, too, are sometimes more concerned in moving people on through the rooms than in allowing them to enjoy the pictures at their leisure – I have even seen a man anxious to compare one picture with another in a previous room told that he could not retrace his steps because he had seen '*that* room already'!

The Apartments are entered from the North Terrace and you are recommended to see the room of Old Master drawings (see above for opening hours) *before* proceeding to the apartments. This is a selection from the vast holdings of drawings by Holbein, Michelangelo, Leonardo, Raphael, and others and also contains a delightful case of miniatures including four by Holbein, ten by Hilliard and eight by Oliver. The Apartments' tour proper starts with the ascent of the Grand Staircase, followed by the display of arms under the Gothic vaulting of the Grand Vestibule. The Waterloo Chamber houses the thirty portraits commissioned from Sir Thomas Lawrence by George IV when Prince Regent – Lawrence was sent round Europe by Royal Command to paint all the sovereigns, politicians and generals jointly responsible for the victory of the allies over Napoleon. Lawrence was knighted before he went, and made President of the Royal Academy on his return, so we could hardly expect him to be unflattering when he painted those responsible for his twin elevations. He was however at his best with *Wellington* (top row centre, east wall), *Pope Pius VII* (bottom row extreme right south wall), and *The Archduke Charles of Austria* (fourth from left, top row West Wall over entrance).

The Ante-Throne Room has Zuccarelli's *The Meeting of Isaac and Rebecca* and the Garter Throne Room has, above the Louis XVI lacquered commode, portraits of *Albert, Prince Consort* and *Queen Victoria* by one of their favourite artists, Franz Xavier Winterhalter. Pass through the Grand Reception Room and its Gobelin tapestries into St George's Hall. High on the north wall are portraits of Stuart and Hanoverian monarchs by Kneller (*George I, William III, Mary II, Anne*) Lely (*Charles II, James II*), Van Dyck (*James I* after van Somer) and others. The Queen's Audience Chamber has van Honthorst's *William II of Orange* over the exit door. Beyond this exit door, masterpieces follow thick and fast for the next six rooms. The Queen's Ball Room has four Canalettos grouped in two pairs either side of the fireplace, and another two opposite between the windows together with two Marco Riccis. To the right of the entrance is Gainsborough's *Col. St Leger* and to the far left is J.S. Copley's picture of *George III's youngest daughters* with dogs and a tambourine. The Queen's Drawing Room, on the other hand, is dominated by Sir Anthony Van Dyck. On the wall to the left is his brilliant group portrait of *Charles I's Eldest Children* (with a huge dog larger than the children), and on the other wall, *George Villiers and his brother Francis* (as children, with Villiers in red and his brother in old gold, and as elegant a picture as one could wish), and *Thomas Killigrew and (?) Lord Crofts* (in which Killigrew is young and handsome, rather than the Restoration rake he became), Van Dyck's view of *Henrietta Maria* (in profile), *Mary Villiers*, and *Charles I* are on this wall too.

The King's Closet has five more Canalettos and two in his style, also Claude's *Rape of Europe*. William Hogarth's *David Garrick and his wife* is over the fireplace (contemporary rumour had it that Hogarth and actor Garrick fell out over the picture), and here, too, is *Garrick as Kitely* by Reynolds (Kitely was a character in Ben Jonson's play *Every Man in his Humour*). The King's State Bedchamber continues at this high quality with (going clockwise) Gainsborough's *Johann Fischer* (if only it could be seen), Zoffany's strange children *Charlotte Princess Royal and William Duke of Clarence*, Canaletto's *Old Library and Church of Santa Maria della Salute*, Zoffany's *Prince of Wales and Duke of York* and Cuyp's very delicately lit *Evening Landscape* with its grey clouds traced in the sky like smoke. If currently on show, Vermeer's *Lady at the Virginal* will probably be here too. The King's Drawing Room features the very large and striking Van Dyck *St Anthony, St Martin dividing his Cloak* on the left-hand wall. Opposite over the fireplace is Rubens' very plebian *Holy Family* and to either side of it are his paired pictures, *Winter Scene: peasants in a barn* and *Summer: a landscape with peasants going to market*.

The last of the State Apartments is the King's Dining room. It features a Verrio ceiling where Ganymede dishes out nectar to the assembled gods at table, and an unusual Kneller *The Chinese Convert*. The Daniel Mytens *Duke of Richmond and Lennox* in the right-hand alcove opposite the entrance cannot, alas, be seen.

7
BOND STREET AND ST. JAMES'S

The Commercial Art Galleries

London is full of galleries selling paintings, prints and sculpture and it would be impossible to cover every one or even most of them here. However, one area stretching from Oxford St to the north to Pall Mall in the south might reasonably be called the heart of the art world. Generally speaking, the galleries, auction and salerooms in the area (see map p.126) are open from 10.00 to 17.30 from Monday to Friday and 10.00 to 13.00 on Saturday. These galleries are open completely free during the course of their current shows, so that a tour around them can serve two purposes – it allows one to buy an original work of art if one's pocket and wallet are sufficiently capacious, or, for the rest of us, it gives a chance to see a cross-section of British and foreign work currently on offer, and that means in advance of its being enshrined in the museums and private collections. Work on show of course varies from the superb and the masterly to the glib, trendy and pretentious (without the prices necessarily differentiating between the two), and each gallery will have its own artists or periods in which it will specialise. With the help of the map and the list which follows, it is hoped the reader will embark on an extended browse for himself (Cork Street is an excellent place to start). However if time is limited and the visits have to be carefully planned, the fortnightly magazine *Arts Review* (available from most good newsagents) always carries full details of current offerings and individual opening hours. Telephone numbers are given in the list below which is arranged alphabetically according to streets, but remember to use the prefix 01 – if telephoning from outside the London area.

Albemarle St

No 2	Parker (Tel: 499-5906)
No 6	Marlborough Fine Art (Tel: 629-5161)
No 11	Christie's Contemporary Art
No 18	Marshall Spink (Tel: 493–2575)
No 38	William Weston, Art Dealer (Tel: 493–0722)
No 38	Cooling gallery (Tel: 629–5224)
No 47	Christopher Drake (Tel: 493–9014)

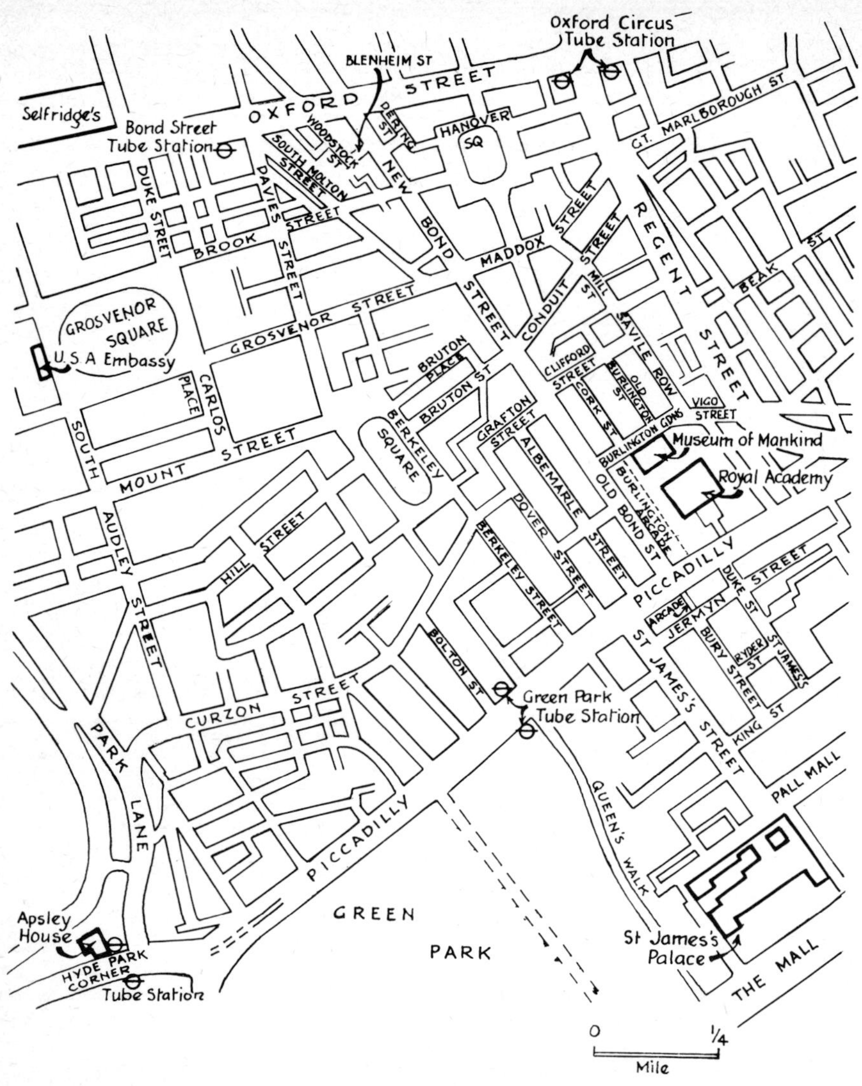

Blenheim St
No 7 Phillips, Auctioneers (Tel: 499–8541)

Brook St
No 24 Brook St Gallery (Tel: 493–1550)

No 31 Acoris Surrealist Art Centre (Tel: 493–3480)
No 31 New Grecian (Tel: 493–3950)
No 33 Stooshnoff Fine Arts (Tel: 629–2052)

Bruton Place
No 31a Rowan (Tel: 493–3727)

Bruton St
No 12 Hugh Moss (Tel: 499–5625)
No 28 Christopher Webb (Tel: 499–0298)
No 29 Rutland (Tel: 629–0303)
No 30 Lefevre (Tel: 629–2250)
No 31 Arthur Tooth and Sons Ltd. (Tel: 499–6741)

Bury St., St James's
No 8 Terry-Engell, art dealer (Tel: 839–2606)
No 11 Malcom Henderson (Tel: 930–2902)
No 38 Gooden and Fox (Tel: 930–6422)

Carlos Place
No 13 O'Hana Gallery (Tel: 499–1562)

Clifford St
No 3 Editions Graphiques (Tel: 734–3944)
No 10 Kasmin (Tel: 437–1645)
No 15a Maas (Tel: 734–2302)

Colville Place, Whitfield St (not on map – just south of Goodge St)
No 1 Curwen (Tel: 636–1459)

Conduit St
No 26 Royal Society of Painters in Watercolour (Tel: 629–8300)
No 45 Helikon Gallery

Cork St
No 2 Waddington I (Tel: 734–1719)
No 3 Maltzahn (Tel: 437–6851)
No 4 Sabin (Tel: 734–6186)
No 8 Hamet (Tel: 437–3922)

No 16 Cork Street Galleries (Tel: 493–0745)
No16a Piccadilly (Tel: 629–2875)
No 19 Roland, Browse and Delbanco (Tel: 734–7984)
No 20 Redfern (Tel: 734–1732)
No 22 John Whibley (Tel: 734–7840)
No 22a Leicester Gallery (Tel: 437–8995)
No 23 Moorland (Tel: 734–6961)
No 25 Victor Waddington, art dealers (Tel: 734–3534)
No 26 Mercury (Tel: 734–7800)
No 34 Waddington II and III (Tel: 439–1866)

D'Arblay St (not on map: off Wardour St)
Nos 20–21 Thumb Gallery (Tel: 439–4059)

Davies St
No 24 Lumley Cazalet (Tel: 499–5058)
No 28 Gallery 43 (Tel: 499–6486)
No 30 Gimpel Fils (Tel: 493–2488)

Dering St
No 9 Anthony D'Offay (Tel: 629–1578)

Dover St
No 18 Ross Galleries (Tel: 629–0975)
No 37 Printmakers Council.
No 41 Tryon (Tel: 493–5161)
No 44 Richard Green (Tel: 493–7997)

Duke St, Grosvenor Square
No 77 Madden (Tel: 493–5854)
No 79 Prudhoe (Tel: 629–6272)

Duke St, St James's
No 6 N.R. Omell (Tel: 839–6223)
No 6 Kaplan (Tel: 930–8665)
No 8 Gerald M. Norman (Tel: 839–7595)
No 13 Leonard Koetser Gallery (Tel: 930–9348)
No 38 Brian Koetser Gallery (Tel: 930–6309)
No 39 Hartnoll and Eyre (Tel: 930–9308)
No 43a M. Newman Ltd (Tel: 930–6068)

plus the Albany Gallery at 14 Mason's Yard, Duke St, St James's (Tel: 839–6119)

Grafton St
No 1a New Grafton (Tel: 499–1800)
No 7 Medici Gallery (Tel: 629–5675)
Nos 9–10 Alwin (Tel: 499–0314)
No 13a Gallery 21 (Tel: 493–6832)
No 16a Portal (Tel: 493–0706)
No 23 Archer Gallery (Tel: 493–2630)

Grosvenor St
No 3b Alexander Postan Fine Art (Tel: 629–0984)
No 8 Achim Moeller (Tel: 493–7611)

Henrietta Place (not on map: north of Oxford St)
No 11 Heller (Tel: 636–8184)

Jermyn St
No 57 Lasson (Tel: 629–6981)
No 59 Heim (Tel: 493–0688)

King St
No 5 Spink and Son Ltd (Tel: 930–7888)
No 8 Christie's Fine Art Auctioneers (Tel: 839–9060)
No 17 Robert Preston (Tel: 930–1794)
No 17 King St Galleries (Tel: 930–3993)
No 30 Fischer Fine Art (Tel: 839–3942)

Maddox St
No 29 Kinsman and Morrison (Tel: 499–9849)

Mount St
No 119 Trafford (Tel: 499–2021)

New Bond St
No 4 Frank Sabin (Tel: 499–5553)
No 8 John Mitchell and Sons (Tel: 493–7567)
No 22 London Arts Gallery (Tel: 493–0646)
Nos 34–5 Sotheby and Co. Auctioneers (Tel: 493–8080)

No 36	William Darby (Tel: 629–3108)
No 41	Frost and Reed (Tel: 629–2457)
No 123	Fores (Tel: 629–5319)
No 147	Wildenstein (Tel: 629–0602) ✓
No 148	Fine Art Society (Tel: 629–5116)
No 173	Baskett and Day (Tel: 629–2991)

Plus Richard Kruml at 9, Lancashire Court, New Bond St (Tel: 629–3017)

Old Bond St

No 13	Leger (Tel: 629–3538) ✓
No 14	Colnaghi's (Tel: 493–1943) ✓
Nos 17–18	Marlborough Graphics (Tel: 629–5161)
No 28	Arcade (Tel: 493–1879)
No 39	Marlborough (Tel: 629–5161)
No 43	Agnew's (Tel: 629–6176)

Piccadilly Arcade

No 9	Ferrers (Tel: 493–6948)

Portland Mews, D'Arblay St (see *D'Arblay St*)

Nos 3–4	Angela Flowers (Tel: 734–0240)

Ryder St

Nos 1–3	M. Newman (Tel: 930–6068)
No 4	Hazlitt (Tel: 930–6821)
No 6	Hal O'Nian's Gallery (Tel: 930–9392)
No 10	Appleby Brothers (Tel: 930–2209)
No 21	M. Bernard (Tel: 930–6894)

St James's St

No 24	Brod (Tel: 839–3871)
No 39	Leggatt Brothers, Art Dealers (Tel: 930–3772)

Savile Row

No 16	Felicity Samuel (Tel: 734–8557)

South Audley St

No 62	Herner Wengraf Ltd, Old Masters Galleries (Tel: 629–0223)

No 74 Alpine Gallery (Tel: 499–1654)

South Moulton St
No 14 Mayor (Tel: 493–8778)
No 21 Electrum (Tel: 629–6325)
No 48 Grosvenor (Tel: 629–0891)

Tottenham Mews (not on map: near the Middlesex Hospital)
Nos 11–12 Annely Juda Fine Art (Tel: 580–7593)

Woodstock St
No 16 Woodstock (Tel: 629–4419)

APPENDICES

I Some Art Bookshops

For those whose pockets rise to neither an original painting nor a limited edition print, the following is a list of some bookshops who either have a large selection of new art-books, or who deal in antiquarian books of art interest.

Arts Council shop, 28 Sackville St, W.1. (Tel: 734–4318)
Louis W. Bondy, 16 Little Russell St, W.1. (Tel: 405–2733)
Paul Breman Ltd, 1 Rosslyn Hill, N.W.3. (Tel: 435–7730)
Dillon's University Bookshop Ltd, 1 Malet St, W.C.1. (Tel: 637–1577)
Fisher and Sperr, 46 Highgate High St, N.6. (Tel: 340–7244)
Foyle's, 119 Charing Cross Rd, W.C.2. (Tel: 437–5660)
Hatchard's, 187 Piccadilly, W.1. (Tel: 734–3201)
London Art Book Shop, 72 Charlotte St, W.1. (Tel: 636–8565)
Marlborough Rare Books Ltd, 35 Old Bond Street, W.1. (Tel: 493–6993)
J.F.T. Rodgers and Co, 34 Bruton Place, W.1. (Tel: 493–3859)
St George's Gallery Books Ltd, 8 Duke St, St James's S.W.1. (Tel: 930–0935)
E. Seligmann, 25 Cecil Court, W.C.2. (Tel: 836–1380)
A. Zwemmer, 76–80 Charing Cross Rd, W.C.2. (Tel: 836–4710)

2 Artists Represented in London Collections

Note: The following list of artists is not comprehensive for such a catalogue would fill many volumes. It should however assist you to locate the main places of interest in and around London for every major artist and for the majority of the minor ones. So that the list shall have maximum value for reference, entries have been included here even if there has been no space to mention the artist in every relevant individual museum and gallery account in the main text. Similarly, if there is one work by an artist in a church or other public building not otherwise worth individual attention in the main text, the place has been included in the list here in brackets. Also, in view of the vast holdings of some major institutions (e.g. The British Museum, The Victoria and Albert Museum, and The Tate Gallery) and their policy of continuous acquisition, it is always worth checking with them for a particular artist whether or not an entry is included in the list below.

ALBERS, Josef
(1888–) Tate.

ALBERTINELLI, Mariotto
(1474–1515) Courtauld.

ALMA-TADEMA, Sir Lawrence
(1836–1912) Tate, Leighton House, Victoria & Albert, William Morris House.

ALTDORFER, Albrecht
(Before 1480–1538) National Gallery.

AMIGONI, Jacopo
(1682–1752) National Portrait Gallery.

ANGELICO, Fra
(c. 1387–1455) National Gallery.

ANNIGONI, Pietro
National Portrait Gallery.

ANTONELLO da Messina
(c. 1430–1479) National Gallery.

APPEL, Karel
(1921–) Tate.

APT, Ulrich
(c. 1456–1532) Hampton Court.

ASHFIELD, Edmund
(active 1670–1700) Ham House.

AUERBACH, Frank
(1931–) Tate.

AVERCAMP, Hendrick
(1585–1634) National Gallery, Windsor (drawings).

BACON, Francis
(1909–) Tate.

BALDOVINETTI, Alesso
(c. 1426–99) National Gallery.

BALDUNG, Hans
(c. 1484/5–1545) National Gallery.

BARLOW, Francis
(1626?–1702) Ham House.

BALLA, Giacomo
(1874–1958) Tate.

BARRINGTON, Mrs Russell
Leighton House.

BARRY, James
(1741–1806) Tate.

BARTOLOMMEO, Martino di

(active 1389–1435) Courtauld.

BARTOLOMMEO Veneto
(active 1502–1546) National Gallery, Wallace.

BASSANO, Jacopo
(c. 1510–1542) National Gallery, Victoria & Albert, Ham House, Hampton Court.

BAYES, Walter
(1869–1956) Imperial War Museum.

BEALE, Charles
(1660–after 1693) Victoria & Albert.

BEARDSLEY, Aubrey
(1872–1898) Tate, Victoria & Albert, British Museum.

BECCAFUMI, Domenico di Pace called
(1484–1551) National Gallery, Victoria & Albert.

BEGA, Abraham Jansz Begeyn called,
(1637–1697) Ham House.

BELL, Vanessa
(1879–1961) National Portrait Gallery, Tate, Courtauld.

BELLINI, Gentile
(c. 1429–1507) National Gallery.

BELLINI, Giovanni
(1430/40–1516) National Gallery, Courtauld, Hampton Court.

BERCHEM, Nicholaes
(1620–1683) National Gallery, Gallery, Wallace.

BERGOGNONE, Ambrogio
(active 1481–1523) National Gallery.

BEVAN, Robert
(1865–1925) Tate.

BEWICK, Thomas
(1753–1828) British Museum, Tate.

BLAKE, Peter
(1932–) Tate, Victoria & Albert.

BLAKE, William
(1757–1827) Victoria & Albert, British Museum.

BOCCIONI, Ugo
(1882–1916) Tate.

BOL, Ferdinand
(1618–1680) National Gallery, Wallace.

BOLTRAFFIO, Giovanni
(1466–1516) National Gallery.

BOMBERG, David
(1890–1957) National Portrait Gallery, Tate.

BONINGTON, Richard Parkes
(1801–1828) Tate, Victoria & Albert, Wallace.

BONNARD, Pierre
(1867–1947) Tate, Courtauld.

BOSCH, Hieronymus
(c. 1450– c. 1516) National Gallery.

BOTH, Jan
(c. 1618–1652) National Gallery, Wallace.

BOTTICELLI, Sandro
(c. 1445–1510) National Gallery, Courtauld.

BOUCHER, Francois
(1703–1770) National Gallery, Victoria & Albert, Wallace, Kenwood, Dulwich.

BOUDIN, Eugene
(1825–1898) National Gallery.

BOURSSE, Esaias
(1631–1672) Wallace.

BOUTS, Dieric
(active c. 1448–1475) National Gallery.

BRAMANTINO, Bartolomeo
(c. 1466–1536) National Gallery.

BRANGWYN, Sir Frank
(1867–1956) Tate, Imperial War Museum, William Morris House, (mural in Royal Exchange).

BRAQUE, Georges
(1882–1963) Tate.

BRATBY, John
(1928–) Tate.

BREENBERGH, Bartholomeus

(1599–1656?) National Gallery, Ham House.

BRETT, John
(1830–1902) Tate.

BRILL, Paul
(1554–1626) Apsley House.

BRONZINO, Agnolo
(1503–1572) National Gallery, Wallace.

BROUWER, Adriaen
(1605/6–38) National Gallery, Victoria & Albert, Wallace, Dulwich.

BROWN, Ford Madox
(1821–1893) National Portrait Gallery, Tate, Leighton House, Victoria & Albert, William Morris House.

BRUEGHEL, Jan (the elder)
(1568–1625) National Gallery, Apsley House, Victoria & Albert.

BRUEGHEL, Pieter (the elder)
(c. 1525–1569) National Gallery, Hampton Court.

BUFFET, Bernard
(1928–) Tate.

BURGESS, John Bagnold
(1830–1897) Royal Holloway College.

BURNE-JONES, Sir Edward Coley
(1833–1898) Tate, Leighton House, Victoria & Albert.

BURRA, Edward
(1905–) Tate.

CALDARA, Polidoro
(Died 1543) Hampton Court.

CAMPIN, Robert
(1378–1444) National Gallery.

CANALETTO, (orig.) Giovanni Antonio Canal
(1697–1765) National Gallery, Victoria & Albert, Soane, Wallace, Dulwich, Greenwich, Windsor.

CAPPELLE, Jan Van De
(c. 1624–1679) National Gallery, Kenwood.

CARAVAGGIO, Michelangelo da
(1573–1610) National Gallery, Hampton Court.

CARPACCIO, Vittore
(active 1490–1523/6) National Gallery.

CARLILE, Joan
(1606?–1679) Ham House.

CARR, Henry
(1894–1970) Imperial War Museum.

CARRA, Carlo
(1888–1966) Tate.

CARRACCI, Annibale
(1560–1609) National Gallery.

CASALI, Andrea
(active around 1750?) Syon House.

CESARE, Guiseppe
(1568–1640) Apsley House.

CEZANNE, Paul
(1839–1906) National Gallery, Tate, Courtauld.

CHAGALL, Marc
(1889–) Tate.

CHAMPAIGNE, Philippe De
(1602–1674) National Gallery, Wallace, Hampton Court.

CHARDIN, Jean Baptiste Simeon
(1699–1779) National Gallery.

CIMA, Giovanni Battista
(1459/60–1517/8) National Gallery, Wallace.

CIPRIANI, Giovanni Battista
(1727–1785) Syon House.

CLAUDE Gelle or Le Lorrain
(1600–1658) National Gallery, Apsley House, British Museum (drawings), Wallace, Dulwich.

CLEYN, Francis
(1582–1658) Ham House, (Somerset House).

CLOUET, Jean
(active 1516–1540) Windsor Castle.

COELLO, Claudio
(1630/35–1693) Apsley House.

COLE, Leslie
(1910–) Imperial War Museum.
COLLINSON, James
(1825–1881) Tate.
COLQUHOUN, Robert
(1914–1962) Tate.
CONDER, Charles
(1868–1909) National Portrait Gallery, Tate, William Morris House.
CONSTABLE, John
(1776–1837) National Gallery, Tate, Victoria & Albert, Fenton House, Ham House, Royal Holloway College, (Royal Academy, Guildhall).
COOPER, Samuel
(1609–1672) National Portrait Gallery, Victoria & Albert, Ham House, Windsor Castle.
COPLEY, John Singleton
(1738–1815) National Portrait Gallery, Tate, Windsor Castle.
COROT, Jean Baptiste Camille
(1796–1875) National Gallery, Victoria & Albert, Wallace.
CORREGGIO, Antonio
(1489–1534) National Gallery, Apsley House, Courtauld, Hampton Court.
COSSA, Francesco Del
(c. 1435–c. 1477) National Gallery.
COTMAN, John Sell
(1782–1842) Tate, Victoria & Albert.
COURBET, Gustave
(1819–1877) National Gallery, Victoria & Albert.
COZENS, Alexander
(c. 1717–1786) Tate, Victoria & Albert.
COZENS, John Robert
(1752 1797) Tate, Victoria & Albert.
CRANACH, Lucas (the Elder)
(1472–1553) National Gallery, Courtauld, Hampton Court.
CRANE, Walter
(1845–1915) William Morris House, Victoria & Albert.
CRIPPA, Roberto
(1921–) Tate.
CRIVELLI, Carlo
(1457–1493) National Gallery, Victoria & Albert, (St Augustine's Church, Kilburn).
CRIVELLI, Vittore
(active c. 1480–c. 1500) Victoria & Albert.
CROME, John
(1768–1821) Tate, Victoria & Albert, Kenwood, Royal Holloway College.
CROSSE, Lawrence
(died 1724) Victoria & Albert.
CUYP, Albert
(1620–1691) National Gallery, Wallace, Kenwood, Dulwich, Windsor Castle.

DADD, Richard
(1817–1887) Tate.
DADDI, Bernardo
(active 1312–1348) Courtauld, Wallace, Hampton Court.
DAHL, Michael
(1659–1743) National Portrait Gallery, National Maritime Museum.
DALI, Salvador
(1904–) Tate.
DANBY, Francis
(1793–1861) Tate, Victoria & Albert, Soane, (Bethnal Green Museum).
DA SALIBA, Antonello
(?1480–1535) Victoria & Albert.
DAUMIER, Honoré
(1808–1874) National Gallery, Victoria & Albert, Courtauld.
DAVID, Gerard
(active 1484–1525) National Gallery.

DAVIE, Alan
(1920–) Tate.
DA VINCI,
(see under Leonardo)
DEGAS, Edgar
(1834–1917) National Gallery, Tate, Victoria & Albert, Courtauld.
DE KOONING, Willem
(1904–) Tate.
DELACROIX, Ferdinand Victor Eugene
(1798–1863) National Gallery, Victoria & Albert, Wallace.
DELAROCHE, Hippolyte (known as Paul)
(1797–1856) Wallace.
DE LA TOUR, Georges
(1593–1652) Hampton Court.
DELAUNAY, Robert
(1885–1941) Tate.
DE LOUTHERBOURG, Philippe
(1740–1812) Tate, Victoria & Albert, Greenwich.
DELVAUX, Paul
(1897–) Tate.
DERAIN, Andre
(1880–1954) Tate.
DE STAËL, Nicolas
(1914–1955) Tate.
DEVERELL, Walter Howell
(1827–1854) Tate.
DE WINT, Peter
(1784–1849) Victoria & Albert.
DI CHIRICO, Giorgio
(1888–) Tate.
DIXON, Nicholas
(active 1660–1708) Victoria & Albert.
DOBSON, William
(1610–1646) Chiswick House.
DOMENICHINO, Domenico Zampieri known as
(1581–1641) National Gallery, Wallace, Dulwich, Hampton Court, Windsor Castle.
DORÉ, Gustav
(1832–1883) Victoria & Albert.
DOSSI, Dosso
(1474/9–1542) National Gallery, Hampton Court.
DOU, Gerrit
(1613–1675) National Gallery, Wallace, Hampton Court.
DUBUFFET, Jean
(1901–) Tate.
DUCCIO Di Buoninsegna
(active 1278–1319) National Gallery, Hampton Court.
DUCHAMP, Marcel
(1887–1968) Tate.
DUFY, Raoul
(1877–1953) Tate, Courtauld.
DUGHET, Gaspard
(1615–1675) see Poussin
DURER, Albrecht
(1471–1528) National Gallery, Victoria & Albert, British Museum (drawings), Windsor Castle.
DYCE, William
(1806–1864) Tate (Guildhall, All Saints Church, Margaret St, Houses of Parliament).

EGG, Augustus
(1816–1863) Tate.
ELSHEIMER, Adam
(1578–1610) National Gallery, Apsley House, Dulwich, Hampton Court.
ENSOR, James
(1860–1949) Tate.
ERNST, Max
(1891–) Tate.
ETTY, William
(1787–1849) Tate, Victoria & Albert.
EYCK, Jan Van
(c. 1390–1441) National Gallery.

FABRITIUS, Carel
(1622–1654) National Gallery.
FANTIN-LATOUR, Henri
(1836–1904) National Gallery,

Tate, Victoria & Albert.
FETI, Domenico
(c. 1589–1624) Hampton Court.
FILDES, Sir Luke
(1843–1927) Tate, Royal Holloway College.
FLATMAN, Thomas
(1635–1688) Victoria & Albert.
FOPPA, Vincenzio
(c. 1427–1515) National Gallery, Wallace.
FORAIN, Jean-Louis
(1852–1931) Tate.
FOUQUET, Jean
(1415–c. 1481) British Museum (manuscripts).
FRAGONARD, Jean Honoré
(1732–1806) Wallace.
FRANCIS, Sam
(1923–) Tate.
FREUD, Lucian
(1922–) Tate.
FRITH, William Powell
(1819–1909) Tate, Royal Holloway College.
FROST, Terry
(1915–) Tate.
FUNGAL, Bernardino
(1460–1516) Victoria & Albert.
FUSELI, Henry
(1741–1825) Tate, Victoria & Albert, British Museum (drawings), Soane, (Royal Academy).

GADDI, Agnolo Di Taddeo known as (active 1369–1396) National Gallery.
GAINSBOROUGH, Thomas
(1727–1788) National Gallery, National Portrait Gallery, Tate, Victoria & Albert, Courtauld, Wallace, Kenwood, Dulwich, Syon House, Royal Holloway College, Ham House, Windsor Castle, (Royal Academy).
GAROFALO, Benvenuto Tisio da
(1481–1559) National Gallery, Hampton Court, (Southwark Cathedral).
GAUGUIN, Paul
(1848–1903) National Gallery, Tate, Courtauld.
GEERTGEN Tot Sint Jans
(?1465–1495?) National Gallery.
GELDER, Aert De
(c. 1645–1727) Dulwich.
GENTILE DA FABRIANO,
(c. 1360–1427) Hampton Court.
GERICAULT, Jean Louis Andre Theodore
(1791–1824) National Gallery, Wallace.
GHEERAERTS, Marcus
(c. 1516– before 1604) National Portrait Gallery.
GHIRLANDAIO, Domenico
(c. 1468–1494) National Gallery.
GILL, Colin
(1892–1940) Imperial War Museum.
GILMAN, Harold
(1876–1919) Tate.
GINNER, Charles
(1876–1961) Tate.
GIORDANO, Luca
(1634–1705) National Gallery, Apsley House.
GIORGIONE, (orig.) Giorgio Del Castelfranco
(1475–1510) National Gallery, Courtauld, Hampton Court.
GIOTTO Di Bondone
(c. 1267–1337) followers of, National Gallery, Courtauld.
GIOVANNI Di Paolo
(died 1452) National Gallery.
GIROLAMO Da Cara
(1501–1556) National Gallery.
GIRTIN, Thomas
(1775–1802) Victoria & Albert, Tate.
GORE, Spencer
(1878–1914) Tate.

GOESSART, Jan (also called Mabuse)
(c. 1478–1533/6). National Gallery, Hampton Court.
GOTTLIEB, Adolph
(1903–) Tate.
GOYA, (orig.) Francisco Jose De Goya y Lucientes
(1746–1828) National Gallery, Apsley House, British Museum, Courtauld.
GREAVES, Walter
(1846–1930) Tate.
EL GRECO, (orig.) Domenikos Theotokopulos
(1541–1614) National Gallery.
GREUZE, Jean Baptiste
(1725–1805) Wallace.
GRIMSHAW, John Atkinson
(1836–1893) Tate.
GRIS, Juan
(1887–1927) Tate.
GROSS, Anthony
(1905–) Imperial War Museum.
GUARDI, Francesco
(1712–1793) National Gallery, Wallace.
GUERCINO, Giovanni Francesco Barbieri
(1591–1666) National Gallery, Apsley House, Dulwich, (Lancaster House).
GUIDO Da Siena
(late thirteenth century) Courtauld.
GUTHRIE, Sir James
(1859–1930) National Portrait Gallery.

HALS, Frans
(c. 1588–1666) National Gallery, Wallace, Kenwood.
HAWKER, Edward
(seventeenth century) National Portrait Gallery.
HAYLS, John
(seventeenth century) National Portrait Gallery.
HAYMAN, Francis
(1708–1776) National Portrait Gallery, Thomas Coram Foundation.
HERKOMER, Sir Hubert Von
(1849–1914) National Portrait Gallery, Tate, Leighton House.
HERMAN, Josef
(1912–) Tate.
HERON, Patrick
(1920–) National Portrait Gallery, Tate.
HIGHMORE, Joseph
(1692–1780) Tate, Victoria & Albert.
HILLIARD, Nicholas
(1547–1619) National Portrait Gallery, Victoria & Albert, British Museum, Ham House, Windsor Castle.
HITCHENS, Ivon
(1893–) Tate, (mural for English Folk Dance & Song Society, Regents Park Road).
HOBBEMA, Meindert
(1638–1709) National Gallery, Wallace, Kenwood.
HOCKNEY, David
(1937–) Tate.
HOGARTH, William
(1697–1764) National Gallery, National Portrait Gallery, Tate, Thomas Coram Foundation, Soane, Dulwich, Hogarth House, Greenwich, Windsor Castle, (Lincoln's Inn, St Bartholomew's Hospital).
HOLBEIN, Hans
(1447/8–1543) National Gallery, National Portrait Gallery, Victoria & Albert, Wallace, Hampton Court, Windsor Castle.
HOOGH, Pieter De
(c. 1629–1684+) National Gallery, Apsley House, Wallace.
HOPPNER, John

(1758–1810) Wallace, Kenwood, Osterley Park House.
HORSLEY, John Callcott
(1817–1903) Royal Holloway College.
HOUGHTON, Arthur Boyd
(1836–1875) Tate.
HUGHES, Arthur
(1832–1915) Tate, Victoria & Albert, William Morris House.
HUNT, William Holman
(1827–1910) National Portrait Gallery, Tate, William Morris House, (St Paul's Cathedral).

IBBETSON, Julius Caesar
(1759–1817) Osterley Park House.
INGRES, Jean Dominique Auguste
(1780–1867) National Gallery, Victoria & Albert.
ISENBRANDT, Adriaen
(died 1551) National Gallery, Fenton House.

JOHN, Augustus
(1878–1961) National Portrait Gallery, Tate, Imperial War Museum.
JOHN, Gwen
(1876–1939) National Portrait Gallery, Tate.
JOHNS, Jasper
(1930–) Tate.
JOHNSON, Cornelius
(1593–1664?) Ham House.
JONES, David
(1895–1974) Tate, Victoria & Albert.
JORDAENS, Jacob
(1593–1678) National Gallery, Wallace.

KANDINSKY, Wassily
(1866–1944) Tate.
KAUFFMANN, Angelica
(1740–1807) National Portrait Gallery, Tate, Victoria & Albert, Kenwood, Osterley Park House.
KENT, William
(1685–1748) Chiswick House, Hampton Court.
KELLY, Sir Gerald
(1879–1972) National Portrait Gallery.
KEYSER, Thomas De
(1596/7–1667) National Gallery.
KITAJ, R.B.
(1932–) Tate.
KLEE, Paul
(1879–1940) Tate.
KLIMT, Gustav
(1862–1918) William Morris House.
KLINE, Franz
(1910–1962) Tate.
KNELLER, Sir Godfrey
(?1649–1723) National Portrait Gallery, Victoria & Albert, Chiswick House, National Maritime Museum, Ham House, Hampton Court, Windsor Castle.
KOKOSCHKA, Oskar
(1886–) Tate.
KONINCK, Philips
(1619–1688) National Gallery.

LAMB, Henry
(1883–1960) Imperial War Museum.
LANCRET, Nicolas
(1690–1743) National Gallery, Wallace, Dulwich.
LANDSEER, Sir Edwin
(1802–1873) Tate, Victoria & Albert, Apsley House, Wallace, Kenwood, Royal Holloway College, (Bethnal Green Museum).
LANYON, Peter
(1918–1964) Tate.
LA THANGUE, Henry Herbert
(1859–1929) Tate.
LAWRENCE, Sir Thomas
(1769–1830) National Gallery,

National Portrait Gallery, Tate, Apsley House, Soane, Wallace, Kenwood, Windsor Castle.
LEAR, Edward
(1812–1888) Tate.
LE BRUN, Charles
(1619–1690) Wallace, Dulwich.
LE CORBUSIER, (orig.) Edouard Jeanneret
(1887–1965) Tate.
LEGER, Fernand
(1881–1955) Tate, Victoria & Albert.
LEGROS, Alphonse
(1837–1911) Tate, William Morris House.
LEIGHTON, Lord Frederic,
(1830–1896) Tate, Leighton House, Victoria & Albert, (Royal Exchange).
LELY, Sir Peter
(1618–1680) National Portrait Gallery, Dulwich, Greenwich, Syon House, Hampton Court, (Guildhall).
LE MOINE, Francois
(1688–1737) Wallace.
LE NAIN, Louis
(c. 1543–1648) National Gallery, Victoria & Albert.
LEONARDO Da Vinci
(1452–1519) National Gallery, British Museum, Windsor Castle (drawings).
LESLIE, Charles Robert
(1794–1859) Tate, Victoria & Albert.
LEWIS, John Frederick
(1805–1876) Tate, Leighton House.
LEWIS, Wyndham
(1884–1957) Tate, Victoria & Albert, Imperial War Museum.
LICHTENSTEIN, Roy
(1923–) Tate.
LINNELL, John
(1792–1882) Tate, Victoria & Albert, Royal Holloway College.
LIPPI, Filippino
(c. 1457–1504) National Gallery.
LIPPI, Fra Filippo
(c. 1406–1469) National Gallery.
LISS, Johann
(c. 1595–1629/30) National Gallery.
LOCHNER, Stephan
(active 1442–1451) National Gallery.
LONG, Edwin
(1829–1891) Royal Holloway College.
LONGHI, Pietro
(1702–1785) National Gallery.
LOTTO, Lorenzo
(c. 1480–1556/7) National Gallery, Hampton Court.
LOUIS, Morris
(1912–1962) Tate.
LOWRY, L.S.
(1887–) Tate, Imperial War Museum.
LUCAS VAN LEYDEN
(1494–1533) National Gallery.
LUINI, Bernardino
(c. 1481/2–1532) National Gallery, Courtauld, Wallace.

MABUSE, see Jan Goessart.
MACBRYDE, Robert
(1913–1966) Tate.
MACLISE, Daniel
(1806–1870) Victoria & Albert, Royal Holloway College.
MAES, Nicolaes
(1632–1693) National Gallery, Apsley House, Wallace.
MAGRITTE, René
(1898–1967) Tate.
MAITRE DES MOULINS,
(active 1483–c. 1500) National Gallery.
MANET, Edouard
(1832–1883) National Gallery, Tate, Courtauld.

MANTEGNA, Andrea
(c. 1430/1–1506) National Gallery, Hampton Court.
MARGARITO OF AREZZO, (active 1262) National Gallery.
MARINI, Marino
(1901–1966) Tate.
MARTIN, John
(1789–1854) Tate, Syon House.
MARTINEAU, Robert Braithwaite
(1826–1869) Tate.
MARTINI, Simone
(1284–1384) Courtauld.
MASACCIO, (orig.) Tommaso Giovanni Di Mone
(1401–1427/9) National Gallery.
MASOLINO Da Panicale
(c. 1383–1447) National Gallery.
MASSON, Andre
(1896–) Tate.
MASSYS, Quinten
(1465/6–1530) National Gallery.
MASTER OF BARONCELLI PORTRAITS,
(active c. 1489) Courtauld.
MASTER BERTRAM,
(active 1367–1387) Victoria & Albert.
MASTER OF THE CAPPENBURG ALTAR-PIECE,
(active first half of the 16th century) National Gallery.
MASTER OF THE GAMBIER-PARRY NATIVITY,
(active first half of the 14th century) Courtauld.
MASTER OF LIESBORN,
(active c. 1464) National Gallery.
MASTER OF THE LIFE OF THE VIRGIN,
(active c. 1463–1480) National Gallery.
MASTER OF S. FRANCESCO,
(active 1290–1305) National Gallery.
MASTER OF ST GILES,
(active c. 1500) National Gallery.
MASTER OF SAN MINIATO,
(active late 15th century) Courtauld.
MASTER OF THE ST URSULA LEGEND (COLOGNE),
(active Cologne c. 1480–1510) Victoria & Albert.
MASTER OF THE ST URSULA LEGEND (FLEMISH),
Victoria & Albert.
MATISSE, Henri
(1864–1954) Tate.
MATTEO Di Giovanni
(died 1495) National Gallery.
MAURIER, George du
(1834–1896) National Portrait Gallery.
MEISSONIER, Jean Louis Ernest
(1815–1891) Wallace.
MEMLINC, Hans
(1430/5–1494) National Gallery, Wallace, Windsor Castle.
MENINSKY, Bernard
(1891–1950) Imperial War Museum.
MERRITT, Anna Lea
(1844–1893) Leighton House.
METSU, Gabriel
(1629–1666) National Gallery, Wallace.
MICHAELANGELO Buonarroti
(1475–1564) National Gallery, Victoria & Albert, British Museum (drawings).
MIDDLEDITCH, Edward
(1923–) Tate.
MILLAIS, Sir John Everett
(1829–1896) National Portrait Gallery, Tate, Leighton House, Victoria & Albert, Thomas Coram Foundation, Royal Holloway College, (Guildhall).
MILLET, Jean Francois
(1814–1875) National Gallery, Victoria & Albert.
MINTON, John
(1917–1957) National Portrait

Gallery, Tate.
MIRO, Joan
(1893–) Tate.
MODIGLIANI, Amedeo
(1884–1920) Tate, Courtauld.
MONACO, Lorenzo
(c. 1370–1425) Courtauld.
MONDRIAN, Piet
(1872–1944) Tate.
MONET, Claude
(1840–1926) National Gallery, Tate, Courtauld.
MONTAGNA, Bartolomeo
(c. 1450–1523) National Gallery.
MOORE, Henry
(1898–) Tate, Victoria & Albert.
MORETTO da Brescia, Allessandro
(c. 1498–1554) National Gallery.
MORISOT, Berthe
(1841–1895) National Gallery, Tate.
MORLAND, George
(1763–1804) Tate, Victoria & Albert, Wallace, Kenwood, Royal Holloway College.
MORONI, Giovanni Battista
(c, 1520/5–1578) National Gallery.
MORRIS, William
(1834–1896) Tate, Victoria & Albert, William Morris House.
MOTHERWELL, Robert
(1915–) Tate.
MOYNIHAN, Rodrigo
(1910–) Tate.
MULREADY, William
(1786–1863) Tate, Victoria & Albert, (Bethnal Green Museum).
MUNCH, Edvard
(1863–1944) Tate.
MURILLO, Bartholomé Esteban
(1617–1682) National Gallery, Apsley House, Wallace, Dulwich.
MYTENS, Daniel
(c. 1590–1642) National Portrait Gallery, National Maritime Museum, Windsor Castle.

NARDO Di Cione
(?c. 1343–1366) National Gallery, Victoria & Albert.
NASH, John
(1893–) Tate, Imperial War Museum.
NASH, Paul
(1889–1946) Tate, Victoria & Albert, Imperial War Museum.
NEER, Aert Van Der
(1604–1677) Wallace, Apsley House.
NEVINSON, C.R.W.
(1889–1946) Tate, Imperial War Museum.
NEWMAN, Barnett
(1905–) Tate.
NICHOLSON, Ben
(1894–) Tate.
NOLAN, Sidney
(1917–) Tate.
NOLAND, Kenneth
(1924–) Tate.
NOLDE, Emil
(1867–1956) Tate, Victoria & Albert.

OLDENBURG, Claes
(1929–) Tate.
OLIVER, Isaac
(1551–1617) National Portrait Gallery, Victoria & Albert, Ham House, Windsor Castle.
OLIVER, Peter
(1594–1647) Victoria & Albert, Wallace, Windsor Castle.
ORCAGNA, (style of)
(active 1344–1368) National Gallery.
ORPEN, Sir William
(1878–1931) National Portrait Gallery, Imperial War Museum.
OUDRY, Jean Baptiste
(1686–1755) Wallace.

PACHER, Michel
(active 1465?–1498) National

Gallery.
PALMER, Samuel
(1805–1851) Tate, Victoria & Albert, British Museum (drawings), (Bethnal Green Museum).
PAOLOZZI, Eduardo
(1924–) Tate.
PARMIGIANINO, Francesco
(1503–1540) National Gallery, Hampton Court.
PASMORE, Victor
(1908–) Tate.
PATENIER, Joachim
(pre 1500–1524) National Gallery.
PATER, Jean Baptiste Joseph
(1696–1736) Wallace, Kenwood.
PATON, David
(active 1660–1695) Ham House.
PERMEKE, Constant
(1886–1951) Tate.
PERUGINO, Pietro Vanucci
(c. 1445/50–1523) National Gallery.
PESELLINO, Francesco
(1422–1457) National Gallery, Courtauld.
PETTIE, John
(1839–1893) Royal Holloway College.
PHILLIPS, Peter
(1939–) Tate.
PHILLIPS, Tom
(1939–) Tate.
PICABIA, Francis
(1879–1953) Tate.
PICASSO, Pablo
(1881–1973) Tate.
PIERO Di Cosimo
(c. 1462–1521?) National Gallery, Dulwich.
PIERO Della Francesca
(c. 1410/20–1492) National Gallery.
PINTURICCHIO, Bernardino
(c. 1454–1513) National Gallery.
PIPER, John
(1903–) Tate, Imperial War Museum, (BBC TV Centre, Wood Lane – wall mosaic, Mayfair Theatre – revolving lantern).
PISANELLO, Antonio
(c. 1395–c. 1455) National Gallery.
PISSARRO, Camille
(1830–1903) National Gallery, Tate, Courtauld.
POELENBURGH, Cornelis Van
(1586?–1667) National Gallery, Apsley House.
POLIAKOFF, Serge
(1906–) Tate.
POLLAIUOLO, Antonio & Piero Del
(c. 1432–1498) & (c. 1441–before 1496) National Gallery.
POLLOCK, Jackson
(1912–1956) Tate.
PONTORMO, Jacopo
(1494–1557) National Gallery.
POTTER, Paulus
(1625–1654) National Gallery, Wallace.
POURBUS, Pieter
(1513–1584) Wallace.
POUSSIN, (orig.) Gaspard Dughet
(1615–1675) National Gallery, Wallace, Osterley Park House.
POUSSIN, Nicolas
(1594–1665) National Gallery, Victoria & Albert, Wallace, Dulwich.
POYNTER, Sir Edward John
(1836–1919) Tate, Leighton House (Guildhall).
PRINSEP, Valentine Cameron (Val)
(1838–1904) Leighton House.
PROVOST, Jan
(c. 1465–1529) Hampton Court.

RAEBURN, Sir Henry
(1756–1823) Tate, Osterley Park House.

RAMSAY, Allan
(1713–1784) National Portrait Gallery, Tate, Thomas Coram Foundation, Wallace, Osterley Park House (attributed).
RAPHAEL, (orig.) Raphaello Sanzio
(1483–1520) National Gallery, Victoria & Albert, Thomas Coram Foundation, Soane, Dulwich, Windsor Castle (drawings).
RAUSCHENBERG, Robert
(1925–) Tate.
RAY, Man
(1890–) Tate.
REDON, Odilon
(1840–1916) Tate.
REMBRANDT Van Rijn
(1606–1669) National Gallery, Victoria & Albert, British Museum (drawings), Wallace, Kenwood, Dulwich, Windsor Castle.
RENI, Guido
(1575–1642) National Gallery, Apsley House, Dulwich, Chiswick House.
RENOIR, Pierre-Auguste
(1841–1919) National Gallery, Tate, Courtauld.
REYNOLDS, Sir Joshua
(1723–1792) National Gallery, National Portrait Gallery, Tate, Apsley House, Victoria & Albert, Thomas Coram Foundation, Soane, Wallace, Kenwood, Dulwich, Greenwich, Syon House, Ham House, Osterley Park House, Windsor Castle, (Guildhall).
RIBERA, José (Jusepe) De also called Il Spagnoletto
(1591–1652) National Gallery, Apsley House.
RICCI, Sebastiano
(1658–1734) National Gallery, Dulwich, Chiswick House, Hampton Court.
RICHARDS, Ceri
(1903–1971) National Portrait Gallery, Tate.
RICHMOND, George
(1809–1896) National Portrait Gallery, Tate.
RICHMOND, Sir William Blake
(1842–1921) National Portrait Gallery.
RILEY, Bridget
(1931–) Tate, Victoria & Albert.
RIVERA, Diego
(1886–1957) Tate.
RIVIÈRE, Briton
(1840–1920) Royal Holloway College.
ROBERTS, William
(1895–) National Portrait Gallery, Tate, Imperial War Museum.
ROMANINO, Girolamo
(1484–1566) National Gallery.
ROMANO, Guilio
(1492–1546) National Gallery, Hampton Court.
ROMNEY, George
(1734–1802) National Gallery, National Portrait Gallery, Tate, Courtauld, Kenwood, Dulwich, Osterley Park House.
ROSA, Salvator
(1615–1673) National Gallery, Apsley House, Wallace, Dulwich.
ROSSETTI, Dante Gabriel
(1828–1882) National Portrait Gallery, Tate, Victoria & Albert, British Museum (drawings), William Morris House.
ROTHENSTEIN, Sir William
(1872–1945) National Portrait Gallery, Tate, Imperial War Museum, Windsor Castle, (RAF Museum, Hendon).
ROTHKO, Mark
(1903–) Tate.
ROUAULT, Georges
(1871–1958) Tate.
ROUSSEAU, Henri
(1844–1910) National Gallery,

Tate, Courtauld.

ROUSSEAU, Pierre Etienne Theodore
(1812–1867) National Gallery, Wallace.

ROWLANDSON, Thomas
(1756–1827) Tate, Victoria & Albert, British Museum (drawings).

RUBENS, Sir Peter Paul
(1577–1640) National Gallery, National Portrait Gallery, Banqueting House, Apsley House, Victoria & Albert, Courtauld, Wallace, Windsor Castle.

RUISDAEL, Jacob Van
(1628–1682) National Gallery, Wallace, Dulwich.

SALIBA, Antonio De
(?1467–after 1535) Victoria & Albert.

SANDBY, Paul
(1725–1809) Tate, Victoria & Albert, Fenton House.

SARGENT, John Singer
(1856–1925) National Portrait Gallery, Tate, Imperial War Museum, (Cliveden).

SARTO, Andrea Del
(1486–1530) National Gallery, Wallace, Hampton Court, Windsor.

SASSETTA, (orig.) Stefano di Giovanni
(c. 1392–1450) National Gallery.

SASSOFERRATO, (orig.) Giovanni Salvi
(1605–1685) National Gallery, Apsley House, Wallace.

SCHOONJANS, Anthonie
Chiswick House.

SCHWITTERS, Kurt
(1887–1948) Tate.

SCOTT, William Bell
(1811–1890) Tate, William Morris House.

SCROTS, William
(active c. 1537–1553) National Portrait Gallery.

SEGHERS, Daniel
(1590–1661) Dulwich, Hampton Court.

SEGHERS, Hercules
(about 1590–1638) National Gallery.

SEGNA Di Bonaventura
(1298–1326) National Gallery.

SEURAT, Georges
(1859–1891) National Gallery, Tate, Courtauld.

SEVERINI, Gino
(1883–1966) Tate.

SHIELDS, Frederick J.
(1833–1911) William Morris House.

SICKERT, Walter
(1860–1942) National Portrait Gallery, Tate.

SIGNAC, Paul
(1863–1935) Courtauld.

SIGNORELLI, Luca
(c. 1441–1523) National Gallery.

SIMS, Charles
(1873–1928) Imperial War Museum.

SISLEY, Alfred
(1839–1899) National Gallery, Tate, Courtauld.

SITTOW, Michel
National Portrait Gallery.

SMITH, Sir Matthew
(1879–1959) Tate.

SNYDERS, Frans
(1579–1657) Wallace, Kenwood.

SODOMA, Giovanni
(1477–1549) National Gallery.

SOLARIO, Andrea
(active 1493–1515/20) National Gallery, Wallace (attributed).

SOLIMENA, Francesco
(1657–1747) National Gallery.

SOLOMON, Solomon Joseph
(1860–1927) Leighton House.

SOULAGES, Pierre
(1919–) Tate.
SOUTINE, Chaim
(1894–1943) Tate.
SPRANGER, Bartholomeus
(1546–1611) National Gallery.
SPENCER, Sir Stanley
(1891–1959) Tate, Imperial War Museum.
STANFIELD, Clarkson
(1793–1867) Tate, Wallace, Royal Holloway College, (Royal Academy, Kensington Palace, Bethnal Green Museum).
STEEN, Jan
(1625/6–1674) National Gallery, Apsley House, Wallace.
STEER, Philip Wilson
(1860–1942) National Portrait Gallery, Tate, Imperial War Museum.
STELLAERT, Jacques (also called Stella)
(1596–1657) Ham House.
STEVENS, Alfred
(1818–1875) Tate, Leighton House.
STILL, Clyfford
(1904–) Tate.
STORCK, Abraham
(1644–later than 1704) Apsley House.
STROZZI, Bernardo
(1581–1644) National Gallery.
STUBBS, George
(1724–1806) National Gallery, National Portrait Gallery, Tate, Fenton House, Kenwood, Windsor Castle.
SUTHERLAND, Graham
(1903–). Tate, Imperial War Museum, (St Aidan's R.C. Church, Acton).

TANGUY, Yves
(1900–1955) Tate.
TAPIES, Antonio
(1923–) Tate.
TENIERS the Younger, David
(1610–1690) National Gallery, Apsley House, Wallace, Dulwich, Hampton Court.
TERBORCH, Gerard
(1617–1681) National Gallery, Wallace.
THORNHILL, Sir James
(1675–1734) National Portrait Gallery, Victoria & Albert, Soane, Greenwich, Hampton Court, (St. Paul's Cathedral, St George's Hanover Square).
TIEPOLO, Giovanni Battista
(1698–1770) National Gallery, Victoria & Albert.
TINTORETTO, Jacopo Robusti
(1518–1594) National Gallery, Leighton House, Courtauld, Hampton Court.
TISSOT, James
(1836–1902) National Portrait Gallery, Tate.
TITIAN, (orig.) Tiziano Vecellio
(active 1511–1576) National Gallery, Courtauld, Wallace, Hampton Court, (St Augustine's Kilburn).
TOBEY, Mark
(1890–) Tate.
TOULOUSE-LAUTREC, Henri De
(1864–1901) National Gallery, Tate, Victoria & Albert (especially for posters), Courtauld.
TREVISANI, Francesco
(1656–1746) Apsley House.
TURA, Cosimo
(c. 1431–1495) National Gallery.
TURNER, J.M.W.
(1775–1851) National Gallery, Tate Gallery, Apsley House, Victoria & Albert, British Museum, Soane, Wallace, Kenwood, Greenwich, Royal Holloway College, (Bethnal Green Museum).

UCCELLO, Paolo
(c. 1397–1475) National Gallery.
UGOLINO Di Nerio
(c. 1317–1327 active till 1339) National Gallery.
UTRILLO, Maurice
(1883–1955) Tate, Courtauld.

VANDERBANK, John
(c. 1694–1739) Ham House.
VAN DE VELDE the Younger
(1633–1707) National Gallery, Apsley House, Wallace, Kenwood, Dulwich, Greenwich, Ham House, Hampton Court.
VAN DYCK, Sir Anthony
(1599–1641) National Gallery, Courtauld, Wallace, Kenwood, Dulwich, Syon House, Hampton Court, Windsor.
VAN GOGH, Vincent
(1853–1890) National Gallery, Tate, Courtauld.
VAN HEEMSKERK, Martin
(1498–1574) Hampton Court.
VAN HONTHORST, Gerrit
(1590–1656) National Gallery, Hampton Court.
VAN HOOGSTRATEN, Samuel
(1627–1678) National Gallery.
VAN HUYSUM, Jan
(1682–1749) National Gallery, Wallace, Dulwich.
VAN LOO, Louis Michel
(1707–1771) Wallace.
VANNUCCIO, Francesco Di
(active c. 1361–1388) Wallace.
VAN SOMER, Paul
(c. 1577–1622) Hampton Court, Windsor Castle.
VASARELY, Victor
(1908–) Tate.
VAUGHAN, Keith
(1912–) Tate.
VAN VEERENDAEL, N.
(1640–1691) Osterley Park House.
VELAZQUEZ, Diego Rodriguez De Silva y
(1599–1660) National Gallery, Apsley House, Wallace.
VERMEER, Jan
(1632–1675) National Gallery, Kenwood, Windsor.
VERNET, Claude Joseph
(1714–1789) National Gallery, Apsley House.
VERONESE, Paolo Caliari
(1528–1588) National Gallery, Courtauld, Dulwich, Hampton Court, (Westminster Hospital, Lancaster House).
VERRIO, Antonio
(1630–1707) Ham House, Hampton House, Hampton Court, Windsor Castle.
VERROCHIO, follower of Andrea Del
(about 1436–1488) National Gallery.
VLAMINCK, Maurice
(1876–1958) Tate.
VOUET, Simon
(1590–1649) National Gallery.
VROOM, Cornelius
(1591–1661) National Gallery, Ham House.
VUILLARD, Edouard
(1868–1940) National Gallery, Tate, Courtauld.

WALLIS, Alfred
(1855–1942) Tate.
WALLIS, Henry
(1830–1916) Tate.
WARD, James
(1769–1859) Tate, Victoria & Albert.
WARHOL, Andy
(?1930–) Tate.
WATERHOUSE, John William
(1849–1917) Tate.
WATTEAU, Antoine
(1684–1721) National Gallery,

British Museum (drawings), Soane, Wallace, Dulwich.

WATTS, George Frederick
(1817–1904) National Portrait Gallery, Tate,Leighton House, Victoria & Albert, Fenton House, (St. Paul's Cathedral, Lincoln's Inn Hall, Watts' Galleries at Compton, Surrey).

WEIGHT, Carel
(1908–) Tate.

WERNER, Joseph
(1637–1710) Victoria & Albert.

WEST, Benjamin
(1738–1820) Tate, Greenwich, Windsor Castle, (Kensington Palace).

WEYDEN, Rogier Van Der
(c. 1399–1464) National Gallery.

WHISTLER, James Abbot McNeill
(1834–1903) National Portrait Gallery, Tate, Leighton House.

WILKIE, Sir David
(1785–1841) Tate, Aspley House, Victoria & Albert, Wallace.

WILLAERTS, Adam
(1577–1664) Greenwich.

WILLIAMSON, Harold Sandys
(1892–) Imperial War Museum.

WILSON, Richard
(1714–1782) National Gallery, Tate, Victoria & Albert, Dulwich, Osterley Park House.

WINDUS, William Lindsay
(1822–1907) Tate.

WINTERHALTER, Franz Xavier
(1806–1873) Windsor Castle.

WORSLEY, John
(1919–) Imperial War Museum.

WOUVERMAN, Philip
(1619–1668) National Gallery, Apsley House, Wallace.

WRIGHT, John Michael
(1617–1700) Banqueting House, Ham House.

WRIGHT of Derby, Joseph
(1734–1797) National Portrait Gallery, Tate, Kenwood.

WYCK, Thomas
(1616–1677) Ham House.

ZINKEISEN, Doris
Imperial War Museum.

ZOFFANY, Johann
(c. 1734–1810) National Gallery, National Portrait Gallery, Tate, Windsor Castle.

ZOPPO, Marco
(c. 1432–c.1478) National Gallery.

ZUCCARELLI, Francesco
(1702–1788) National Gallery, Syon House, Windsor Castle.

ZUCCHI, Antonio
(1726–1795) Osterley Park House.

ZURBARAN, Francisco
(1598–1664) National Gallery.

Index

Apsley House – The Wellington Museum 42
The Banqueting House, Whitehall 22
The Brangwyn Gift 99
The British Museum 63
Chiswick House 98
The Commercial Art Galleries 125
The Thomas Coram Foundation and Foundling Hospital 68
The Courtauld Galleries 73
The Dulwich College Picture Gallery 93
Fenton House 89
The Foundling Hospital 68
Greenwich, The National Maritime Museum 103
Greenwich, The Royal Naval College Painted Hall and Chapel 101
Ham House 106
Hampton Court Palace 115
The Hayward Gallery 89
Hogarth House 97
The Imperial War Museum 87
Institute of Contemporary Arts 22
The Iveagh Bequest, Kenwood 91
Sir John Soane's Museum 69
Kenwood, The Iveagh Bequest 91
Leighton House 48
The London Museum – a special note 47
The Museum of Mankind 41
The National Gallery 1
The National Maritime Museum, Greenwich 103
The National Portrait Gallery 17
Osterley Park House 110
The Queen's Gallery 46
The Royal Academy 41
The Royal Holloway College 113
The Royal Naval College Painted Hall and Chapel 101
St Nicolas' Parish Church 97
Sir John Soane's Museum 69
Syon House 104
The Tate Gallery 29
The Thomas Coram Foundation 68
The Victoria and Albert Museum 53
The Wallace Collection 77
The Wellington Museum, Apsley House 42
William Morris Gallery and Brangwyn Gift 99
Windsor Castle 119